THE GLORY AND PAGEANTRY OF CHRISTMAS

by the Editors of TIME-LIFE Books

Special Edition

Hammond Incorporated

Maplewood, N.J.

Library of Congress Cataloging in Publication Data
Time-Life Books.
    The glory and pageantry of Christmas.
    Originally published as v. 1 and 2 of The Life book
of Christmas, by the editors of Life.
    Includes bibliographies.
    1. Christmas.   I. Life (Chicago).   The Life book
of Christmas.   II. Title.
GT4985.T55 1974   394.2'68282   74-7130
ISBN 0-8437-3751-4

CONTENTS

THE
GLORY
AND
PAGEANTRY
OF
CHRISTMAS

PART ONE

INTRODUCTION

The story of Jesus' birth and of the momentous events of His life was first related by the four Evangelists, who are depicted on the opposite page composing their gospels. At upper left, St. Matthew appears to be pausing in his work to listen to inspirational advice from the angel, the symbol traditionally associated with him. St. Mark, at upper right, turns his head toward the lion, which is his sign. At lower left, St. Luke, attended by the ox, his symbol, is portrayed in deep contemplation. St. John, seen at lower right with his symbolic eagle, is dipping his quill. The stylized portraits of these saints illuminate a gospel book created for the Emperor Charlemagne in the Eighth Century.

Since Charlemagne's artists decorated their New Testament manuscripts, books without end have been written about Christmas. There have been books of great art on the subject of Christmas; books on Christmas traditions; books of stories with a Christmas background; collections of Christmas music, and anthologies, not necessarily *about* Christmas, put together *for* the Christmas season. But no single work exists that brings together the best aspects of all these various books. THE GLORY AND PAGEANTRY OF CHRISTMAS is designed to fill this gap.

Photographers, reporters and researchers, advised by scholars and art historians, searched through the world's great churches, museums and libraries for paintings, literature, sculpture, music, illuminated manuscripts and altarpieces. And they received, in the spirit of Christmas, unexpected gifts from strangers who heard of the book and contributed their favorite Christmas songs and stories.

THE GLORY AND PAGEANTRY OF CHRISTMAS is in two parts. This, the first part, recounts the glory of the Nativity and its fulfillment in terms of Christ's life and His Resurrection. Each of the eight chapters begins with a scriptural passage that introduces the subject. The quotations are taken from the King James version of the Bible because it is so familiar and so revered for its literary quality. Then, in text and reproductions of master paintings and sculpture, the chapters explore the first Christmas, illuminating the lives and times of the participants, tracing the legends (like those of the Three Kings) and the traditions (such as the crèche) that have grown up around the Biblical accounts. The chapters end with an anthology of text and music that sheds additional light on the chapter. These selections come from many sources: historical documents; church music and popular carols; the works of writers great and obscure; the interpretations of scholars and theologians. They also include excerpts from apocryphal texts.

Part Two traces the vivid pageantry of Christmas customs and celebrations since early Christian times.

—THE EDITORS

I
THE PROPHECIES

AND THERE SHALL COME FORTH a rod out of the stem of Jesse, and a Branch shall grow out of his roots: And the spirit of the Lord shall rest upon him, the spirit of wisdom and understanding, the spirit of counsel and might, the spirit of knowledge and of the fear of the Lord; And shall make him of quick understanding in the fear of the Lord: and he shall not judge after the sight of his eyes, neither reprove after the hearing of his ears: But with righteousness shall he judge the poor, and reprove with equity for the meek of the earth: and he shall smite the earth with the rod of his mouth, and with the breath of his lips shall he slay the wicked. . . . The voice of him that crieth in the wilderness, Prepare ye the way of the Lord, make straight in the desert a highway for our God.   ISAIAH, 11:1-4; 40:3

ISAIAH, *whose eloquent voice predicted the coming of Christ, is shown here idealized in baroque grandeur in a German church.*

EXALTED VISION
OF A
MESSIAH
IN THE
HOLY LAND

A 13TH CENTURY PSALTER *from England includes this version of the tree of Jesse with a border decorated with Scriptural scenes.*

GOD'S WORDS were carried to mankind by His servants, the prophets. The prophets who wrote the exalted verses of the Book of Isaiah opening this volume were not the only ones to foretell the coming of a Messiah.

For centuries, the prophets had held before the Hebrews the hope of the coming of an era of holiness and union with God—the "Kingdom of God," as it came to be known—when sin and evil would be destroyed. Israel, the chosen, would be the first to be brought into that kingdom, which from Israel would then spread out until it embraced all the nations of the earth.

At first, the Hebrews looked to the royal family of David, rather than to any one king of the Davidic line, as the earthly agent through which God would set up His kingdom among men. But as king after

king disappointed the expectation of the people, the vision of the prophets turned to one anointed king of David's house, the Messiah, the king of the "End of Days" through whom God would finally and for all time establish the awaited kingdom.

Daniel cried: "I saw in the night visions, and, behold, one like the Son of man came with the clouds of heaven, and came to the Ancient of days, and they brought him near before him. And there was given him dominion, and glory, and a kingdom, that all people, nations, and languages should serve him: his dominion is an everlasting dominion, which shall not pass away, and his kingdom that which shall not be destroyed." And many others—Micah, Jeremiah, Ezekiel, Zechariah, Malachi—said much the same.

As the first Christmas drew near, the people of Israel were held captive once more, this time by the Romans, whose evil agent was Herod. The people yearned for a redeemer who would, they felt sure, deliver them from their tormentor.

In a village just west of Jerusalem, a boy named John was growing up who would soon go into the wilderness to baptize and prepare the people for the coming of the Lord. The land of Canaan stood expectant.

And what was Canaan? A little country of long vistas, tawny colors, delicately molded mountains and a dry, shining light in which to see it all. It was a country for contemplation, a timeless place that invited thoughts on eternity. A man could

stroll its length in a week, walk its breadth in a few days and come to know and love every tree and rock in it, for it stretched only 165 miles, most of it along the eastern shore of the Mediterranean, and reached inland not more than 87 miles.

Behind the sun-washed beaches were fertile plains where grain, vegetables, olives, figs and grapes grew. Eastward, behind the plains, rose mountains intersected by deep gorges and valleys.

This was The Land and in it lived perhaps a half million Jews. Elsewhere in the Roman Empire, some two million more Jews lived and many of them made yearly pilgrimages to Jerusalem, especially at Passover time. Those Jews who lived in the Holy Land were sometimes merchants, rich landowners or skilled craftsmen. But most were farmers and herdsmen. They were proud that King David had been a shepherd and the prophet Amos a "dresser of sycamore trees."

Wherever a Jew turned in this land he found monuments to the splendor of his past. Each holy well, sacred mountain and battlefield was part of the rich tapestry of his history. Scattered about were places which soon would take on new importance: Nazareth, a village so small it is not mentioned in the Old Testament; Bethlehem, a sleepy little herders' town; and Jerusalem—majestic Jerusalem—a city which even on the eve of that first Christmas possessed a thousand years of religious tradition as the city of David and the site of the Temple of Solomon.

THE FAMILY TREE of Jesus in the 13th Century French Psalter of Inge-borg (left) starts with Jesse, reclining at bottom. His line includes David with his "vièle," Solomon with his harp, the Virgin Mary, and Jesus at the top. In descending order at left are prophets Malachi, Daniel and Amos, each bearing his prophecy of the Messiah, and on the right, a sibyl; Ezekiel; and Aaron, brother of Moses and the first high priest of the Jews.

THE VILLAGE OF PEKI'IN *is said, by long tradition, to be the oldest Holy Land community continuou*

A LIFE
OF
VILLAGE WAYS

Most people of the Holy Land lived in little hamlets such as Nazareth or Peki'in, an Upper Galilean village shown above. Those villagers would not feel much out of place should they be returned through time to their former homes. For much of the countryside and many of the small villages remain largely unchanged.

By day the villagers tended farms. By night they rested on their rooftops. And a boy not yet born would later teach: "What ye hear in the ear that preach ye upon the housetops."

habited by Jews. Its houses go back only 200 years, but the carob trees (left center) appeared miraculously, legends say, 1,800 years ago.

HOLY LAND SITES *on the map are Jaffa, from which Jonah sailed; Caesarea, Herod's capital; Bethlehem, where Jesus would be born; Nazareth, where He would grow up; Jericho, near the place of His baptism; Capernaum, where He was to teach; Jerusalem, where He would die and rise again.*

13

PLACID AND SERENE *is the Sea of Galilee,
then as now known as the Sea of Kinneret,
meaning harp-shaped. Here once lived
four boys who would later become Apostles.*

ALONG QUIET SHORES OF SEAS MADE HOLY

Everywhere the waters of the Holy Land evoke the majestic dramas that were long ago played out along their banks. The shores of the Dead Sea *(left)* in the shadowy days of antiquity cradled five "cities of the plain." Two of them had fallen into vile sin, and as Genesis reports: "Then the Lord rained upon Sodom and Gomorrah brimstone and fire. . . ." And near the Dead Sea's shores lived the community of Essene ascetics whose collected writings today are providing new insight into pre-Christian tenets.

Upstream from the Dead Sea, via the winding River Jordan, crossed in their wanderings so many times by the tribes of Israel, was the Sea of Kinneret *(above),* which is really a lake 13 miles long by 6 wide. Its waters are calm, with lake breezes that can turn into sudden storms, buffeting boats about. It teemed with fish. By the time of that first Christmas it was ringed by more settlements than are there today. These villages were full of fishermen and fish picklers. And to one of these hamlets, Capernaum, the boy who would be born in Bethlehem and grow up in Nazareth would come as a grown man. On the hillside and on such shores as the one shown above, He would begin to preach a divine mission that has never ended.

SULLEN AND OPPRESSIVE *are the gravelly shores of the Dead Sea. Pilings mark the site of an
old potash works. No fish can live in these waters, five times saltier than those of the ocean.*

SNOW-TOPPED SLOPES *of Mount Hermon (above) brood on fields of trees and grain. Legend says Hermon's jealous tears, when God met Moses on Mount Sinai, created the River Jordan.*

THE LAND
OF
SACRED LEGEND

This land, this speck in the immensities of the Roman Empire came to haunt the minds of many peoples. A place of barren cliffs, luxuriant valleys, deep defiles and a view of snow-capped peaks, The Land was about to become more: a treasure house sparkling with the truths of the world's yesterdays. In another time the American Negro, caught by holy mysteries, would hauntingly sing, "Oh, way o-ver Jor-dan, view the land, view the land; Way o-ver Jor-dan go view the heav'nly land."

STONY SLOPE *of a hillock near Nazareth (opposite) is where townsmen tried to kill Jesus for chiding them for lacking faith in Him.*

STEEP SLOPES *of the Dishon defile (below) are the corroded product of the small brook at the bottom. This is the land where Barak lived and from here he marched to smite the Canaanites.*

THE OLD, OLD WAR *of man against camel is renewed in a narrow cobblestone street of Bethlehem where an Arab pleads with a beast, loaded with green olive branches, to take one more step.*

THE SONS
OF THE EARTH

The days of the Holy Land went by slowly, so the minutes and hours were ignored. Then, as even now, patient drivers wailed their age-old beseeching cry to the stubborn camel, and in the fields shepherds, young and old alike, guarded their flocks against hyenas, wolves and jackals that roamed the country. Theirs was the basic pastoral life of the Holy Land of old.

The boy who would be born in Bethlehem would watch the shepherds and later, in His mature years, would teach in their images. He would speak of the difficulty of getting camels and rich men through narrow places. And He would speak of the Good Shepherd whose sheep loved him, knew his voice and followed him. He would describe the joy in heaven over a repentant sinner in terms of the joy in a shepherd's heart over the return of a lost sheep. For these were symbols every man in Israel knew and could understand.

THE OLD VIGIL *over the flocks is carried on today near Bethlehem in the same way it was when David tended his sheep on these fields. And David would not have been dressed much differently.*

THE PROPHETS

What manner of men were they who foretold events of the future? Was their prophecy human or divine? Dr. Abraham J. Heschel, an eminent Jewish theologian, explored such questions in "The Prophets" (1962). This excerpt summarizes his thought-provoking answers.

As a witness, the prophet is more than a messenger. As a messenger, his task is to deliver the word; as a witness, he must bear testimony that the word is divine.

The words the prophet utters are not offered as souvenirs. His speech to the people is not a reminiscence, a report, hearsay. The prophet not only conveys; he reveals. He almost does unto others what God does unto him. In speaking, the prophet reveals God. This is the marvel of a prophet's work: in his words, *the invisible God becomes audible.* He does not prove or argue. The thought he has to convey is more than language can contain. Divine power bursts in the words. The authority of the prophet is in the Presence his words reveal.

CRADLE OF THE KINGDOM

Nazareth, home of Joseph and Mary and the town where Jesus grew to manhood, long has attracted writers and artists. This excerpt from "The Life of Jesus," by the noted 19th Century French philosopher Ernest Renan, not only pictures the town and its people but relates them in understandable, contemporary terms to the countryside Jesus came to know and love so well.

Nazareth was a small town in a hollow opening broadly at the summit of the group of mountains which close the plain of Esdraelon on the north. The population is now from three to four thousand, and it can never have varied much. The cold there is sharp in winter, and the climate very healthy. The town, like all the small Jewish towns at this period, was a heap of huts built without style, and would exhibit that harsh and poor aspect which villages in Semitic countries now present. The houses, it seems, did not differ much from those cubes of stone, without exterior or interior elegance, which still cover the richest parts of the Lebanon, and which, surrounded with vines and fig-trees, are still very agreeable. The environs, moreover, are charming; and no place in the world was so well adapted for dreams of perfect happiness. Even in our times Nazareth is still a delightful abode, the only place, perhaps, in Palestine in which the mind feels itself relieved from the burden which oppresses it in this unequaled desolation. The people are amiable and cheerful; the gardens fresh and green. Anthony the Martyr, at the end of the sixth century, drew an enchanting picture of the fertility of the environs, which he compared to paradise. Some valleys on the western side fully justify his description. The fountain, where formerly the life and gaiety of the little town were concentrated, is destroyed; its broken channels contain now only a muddy stream. But the beauty of the women who meet there in the evening—that beauty which was remarked even in the sixth century, and which was looked upon as a gift of the Virgin Mary—is still most strikingly preserved. It is the Syrian type in all its languid grace. No doubt Mary was there almost every day, and took her place with her jar on her shoulder in the file of her companions who have remained unknown. . . . .

The horizon from the town is limited. But if we ascend a little the plateau, swept by a perpetual breeze, which overlooks the highest houses, the prospect is splendid. On the west are seen the fine outlines of Carmel, terminated by an abrupt point which seems to plunge into the sea. Before us are spread out the double summit which towers above Megiddo; the mountains of the country of Schechem, with their holy places of the patriarchal age; the hills of Gilboa, the small, picturesque group to which are attached the graceful or terrible recollections of Shunem and of Endor; and Tabor, with its beautiful rounded form, which antiquity compared to a bosom. Through a depression between the mountains of Shunem and Tabor are seen the valley of the Jordan and the high plains of Paræa, which form a continuous line from the eastern side. On the north, the mountains of Safed, in inclining toward the sea conceal St. Jean d'Acre, but permit the Gulf of Khaïfa to be distinguished. Such was the horizon of Jesus. This enchanted circle, cradle of the kingdom of God, was for years his world. Even in his later life he departed but little beyond the familiar limits of his childhood. For yonder, northward, a glimpse is caught, almost on the flank of Hermon, of Cæsarea-Philippi, his furthest point of advance into the Gentile world; and here southward, the more sombre aspect of these Samaritan hills foreshadows the dreariness of Judea beyond, parched as by a scorching wind of desolation and death.

If the world, remaining Christian, but attaining to a better idea of the esteem in which the origin of its religion should be held, should ever wish to replace by authentic holy places the mean and apocryphal sanctuaries to which the piety of dark ages attached itself, it is upon this height of Nazareth that it will rebuild its temple. There, at the birthplace of Christianity, and in the centre of the actions of its Founder, the great church ought to be raised in which all Christians may worship. There, also, on this spot where sleep Joseph, the carpenter, and thousands of forgotten Nazarenes who never passed beyond the horizon of their valley, would be a better station than any in the world beside for the philosopher to contemplate the course of human affairs, to console himself for their uncertainty, and to reassure himself as to the Divine end which the world pursues through countless falterings. . . .

ECLOGUE IV

Not only the Bible spoke of the coming of a heavenly child. The Roman poet Vergil did so in the poem below, written some 30 years before Jesus' birth. Probably it referred to the heir desired by a noble family, but in the Middle Ages it was taken as a Messianic prophecy.

The last great age, foretold by sacred rimes,
Renews its finished course: Saturnian times
Roll round again; and mighty years, begun
From their first orb, in radiant circles run.
The base degen'rate iron offspring ends;
A golden progeny from heav'n descends.
O chaste Lucina! speed the mother's pains;
And haste the glorious birth!

Jerusalem Gaude

The exultant words of the prophet Zechariah are sung in Seventh Century Gregorian chant at Vespers on "Gaudete" (Rejoice) Sunday in some church liturgies. This service occurs on the second Sunday before Christmas.

Je - ru - sa - lem re - joice, be glad and joy - ful, for___ there___ shall___ come___ un - to thee a Sav - ior, al - le - lu - ia.

II

THE ANNUNCIATION

AND IN THE SIXTH MONTH THE angel Gabriel was sent from God unto a city of Galilee, named Nazareth, To a virgin espoused to a man whose name was Joseph, of the house of David; and the virgin's name was Mary. And the angel came in unto her, and said, Hail, thou that art highly favoured, the Lord is with thee: blessed art thou among women. And when she saw him, she was troubled at his saying, and cast in her mind what manner of salutation this should be. And the angel said unto her, Fear not, Mary: for thou hast found favour with God. And, behold, thou shalt conceive in thy womb, and bring forth a son, and shalt call his name Jesus. . . . And Mary said, Behold the handmaid of the Lord; be it unto me according to thy word. And the angel departed from her. LUKE, 1:26-31, 38

GENTLE VIRGIN *is depicted by Rogier van der Weyden in a detail from the 15th Century Columba altarpiece, now in Munich.*

SIMPLE WORDS,
A COMPLEX
MESSAGE

MARY'S HUMILITY *in the presence of God's messenger is mixed with surprise in this illumination from a 15th Century manuscript.*

TERTULLIAN, one of the early Church fathers, writing of the religious significance of the Annunciation, said: "Eve believed the serpent, Mary believed Gabriel; the one sinned by believing, the other by believing effaced the sin."

Luke, whose unadorned narrative of this supreme event opens this chapter, and the angel Gabriel shared an important talent: In delivering a message, each knew which details to emphasize, which to leave out. The message that Gabriel brought to the Virgin—that she was to "conceive . . . and bring forth a son, and . . . call his name Jesus"—is a message that brought her joy, grief and glory. But Gabriel wasted no words. He left it to Mary's faith, to her intelligence and imagination, to supply the details that he left out. And Mary was equal to the test.

The message that Luke related —the account of the angel Gabriel's Annunciation to Mary—changed the world for all time. But Luke also wasted no words. He concentrated on the essentials and left it to his readers to interpret the message in the light of their faith. Theologians and artists through the ages have accepted Luke's implied invitation and have used his chronicle as the source of inspirations that have enriched the whole of Christendom.

The Annunciation is the beginning of the Christmas story. Theologians assume that the Incarnation —the assumption of human flesh by God in the person of Christ—took place the moment that Mary freely accepted her role by saying to Gabriel: "Be it unto me according to thy word." Thus it is that the Feast of the Annunciation is celebrated March 25, just nine months before Christmas.

Luke's chronicle and the account given from Joseph's viewpoint beginning at Matthew 1:18 are the bases for the doctrine of the Virgin Birth. That doctrine, first authoritatively stated about 150 A.D., is included in both the Nicene and Apostles' Creeds and is held as an article of faith by Roman Catholic and Eastern Orthodox communicants. Beginning in the 19th Century some Protestant liberals rejected the doctrine. However, many Protestants hold to the belief.

On these pages, paintings show Mary and Gabriel in a variety of poses, locales and moods. The very differences point up the universality of Luke's words, the only scriptural account of the Annunciation to Mary. Because Luke set no strictures to restrain them, artists have been free to depict the Annunciation in terms that were both theologically and artistically suited to their civilizations. And, borrowing from apocryphal sources, they developed a rich symbolism that lent deep meaning to their art.

One of the major differences in paintings over the ages is in the status of Mary in relation to Gabriel. In the earliest works, the frescoes of the catacombs of Priscilla in Rome, the Virgin is seated, as though overwhelmed by the news. This is true, also, of works from the early medieval period in which Mary is depicted as humble and submissive. Gabriel, glorious in his kingly robes and carrying a scepter, is the main figure.

After the 14th Century, Mary generally is dominant and the angel is sometimes shown kneeling to her and carrying the lily, her symbol, rather than his own scepter. The change has been attributed to the works of St. Bonaventure, the source of many traditions in Italian art. St. Bonaventure was probably reflecting a growing emphasis in the Church on Mary's exalted position. In other early paintings the Virgin often is depicted as spinning wool and in later paintings as reading holy books.

Luke said nothing about the setting of the scene. Early painters usually placed it in a vaguely defined temple or house, or in a garden patio as in the painting at right. About the same time that Fra Angelico was painting his Annunciation in the early part of the 15th Century, however, a Flemish master believed to be Robert Campin did the famous Merode Altarpiece which is shown on the following pages. This is an early example of a new trend in detailed and realistic interpretation of the Annunciation to Mary in a domestic setting.

The Merode also summarized the learning of centuries in its superb use of symbolism. In the Fra Angelico, for example, the Incarnation is represented by the dove. But in the Merode, each household item holds a symbolic meaning, so that the entire work is permeated with rich allusions to the life of Christ.

GABRIEL'S ANNUNCIATION *is written on this fresco in two lines of Latin, and Mary's answer in one inverted line in between. The Adam and Eve scene (background) is a reminder of original sin, which Jesus will come to expiate. Fra Angelico painted this work about 1430.*

HOLY SIGNS
IN
HOMELY THINGS

The Merode Altarpiece is a triptych, a painting done in three separate panels but meant to be viewed as a single work. It depicts one of the most dramatic moments of the Annunciation, as Mary, unaware of the angel's presence, unaware of the spirit of God, goes on reading. Except for the presence of the angel, the scene might be in any 15th Century Flemish household. But the work is a tour de force of symbolic meaning.

For more than five centuries experts have studied the painting and have read symbolic meanings into many of the commonplace items depicted. In the left panel, the rosebush symbolizes the Crucifixion; the open door, hope; the key represents desire for God. In the center panel, the water basin above Gabriel and the towel beside it signify Mary's purity and cleanliness. Joseph, in his shop in the right panel, is working on a foot warmer or possibly on a spike-board such as the one tied to Jesus on His way to Calvary. In the left panel, the kneeling figures most likely portray the pious donor of the painting and his wife or betrothed.

CHRIST'S ENTRY *into the world carrying the Cross symbolizes His Incarnation and Crucifixion.*

A MOUSETRAP *on Joseph's bench alludes to the concept that Christ's sacrifice trapped the devil.*

EXOTIC OR COMMON, ALL THINGS SPEAK OF JESUS

The richness of the scholarship and imagination of the painter (considered by many art experts to have been Robert Campin) have made the Merode Altarpiece a source of fascination for more than 500 years. Through the use of traditional symbols and his own creations, he infused the painting with a sense of God's presence. Some of the painted metaphors are obvious, some deep and involved.

The traditional symbol for the Incarnation is the presence of the dove of the Holy Ghost. In the Merode detail at top left, Campin painted the Christ Child gliding toward the Virgin on a beam of light that represents the light of God. The passage of the figure through the closed window recalls the comment by St. Bernard on the Virgin Birth that, just as the sun penetrates a glass window without damaging it, "thus the Word of God, the splendor of the Father, entered the virgin chamber and then came forth from the closed womb." The mousetrap at bottom left gives the work its popular title, "The Madonna of the Mousetrap." The trap alludes to a concept of St. Augustine that the human form of Christ fooled the devil as bait fools a mouse. The trap that caught the devil and atoned for the sin of man was the Crucifixion. The tools are emblems of Joseph. The lilies in the pitcher *(opposite)* represent the Virgin's purity. Because a lighted candle symbolizes Christ's divinity, the extinguished candle puzzles scholars. Some hold that the painter meant to show that in the lowly state Christ assumed at the Incarnation, His divinity was concealed by His human form. Another view holds that divine radiance snuffed out the candle.

SYMBOLIC LILIES *suggest Mary's purity. Scholars differ on the meaning of the burned-out candle.*

ON THE ANNUNCIATION OF FRA ANGELICO

As the Annunciation has inspired artists, so their work has moved poets. The painting on page 25 drew from Spain's Manuel Macha-do (1874-1947) this tribute to the artist.

The silver carolling of Matins woke
  The angel artist from his couch to paint,
  While round him throng a rosy chorus quaint
Of cherubs waiting on his brush's stroke.

They guide his hand to set the snowy light
  On Mary's brow and o'er her lovely cheeks
  To show the eyes wherein her pureness speaks,
To limn her slender fingers amber white.

Their angel wings unto his eyes they hold
  So he may copy of their child-like snows
  The plumes of him who brought her message here;
Who rays amid his pearly vestment stoled,
  His light upon the Virgin's breast of rose,
Like vivid sunburst on some crystal sphere.

The Annunciation in Flanders

A compassionate approach to the Annunciation tableau is found in "The Christ Child in Flanders," a retelling of the story by Felix Timmermans (1886-1927). With poetic license but no loss of reverence, the tale unfolds against the background of Flanders in the Middle Ages.

Mary stopped. Glancing up from her heavy breviary, she saw that the sharp sickle of the moon was already hanging in the mother-of-pearl heavens. . . .

Mary buried her nose in the yellow flowers she had arranged in the blue Delft vase on the table and sighed. Delicious longing flooded her heart, making her sit very still and close her eyes. It was the womanly desire to have children, dear gentle children with blonde hair and ruddy cheeks, who in her girlish fancy never grew up, and who would be given her as dew is given the evening meadows.

Mary turned from the window with a sigh. Throwing her blue calico cloak about her shoulders, she took her prayerbook from the mantel and set out to church. As she strode down the birch path her skirts rustled in the stillness.

Then it happened.

Sweetest music blew through the delicate twigs of the birches. Startled, Mary looked up, and when her gaze fell back to the path in front of her, there, woven of evening mists and moonlight, stood an angel of marvelous beauty dressed in cherry-red vestments, a lily in his hand.

Heavenly fire blazed through him, and he glowed like a cathedral window in the sun. With a rush of huge dove's wings he lifted himself from the ground, and an overpowering fragrance as of violets and cloves emanated from him.

It was as though Mary suddenly stood face to face with all she had longed for and been unable to express. Unafraid (though not daring to look into the angel's face) and melting with reverence and humility, she knelt down in the dog-daisies of the path.

Wondrously sweet as no sound ever before heard by human ear, from the throat of the magnificent angel, as though from organ-pipes, rang words of greeting, the message that she was to carry the Lord and was of all women the most blessed, she and the holy fruit of her womb.

Mary dared not ask how this would come about, but the angel sang on: "The Holy Spirit will come upon thee, and the power of the Most High will overshadow thee." There was a silence. Into it, in complete surrender and trembling with happiness, Mary replied: "Behold the handmaid of the Lord; let it be unto me according to thy word." When she raised her head to thank the angel with her eyes, the music faded out of the trees, and there was silence again and evening loneliness, and a heavy fog covering the fields.

When Mary reached the house she forgot to light the lamp and sank weeping upon the table. She wept from an overwhelming joy and the strangeness of her blessing, her tears falling on the yellow flowers.

Outside the heavens stood full of stars.

ANNUNCIATION TO MARY

German writer Rainer Maria Rilke (1875-1926), one of the great modern poets, had a mystical view of God. His fervor shines through this re-creation of the poignant moment when Mary fully realized the presence of the angel.

Not that an angel entered (mark this)
was she startled. Little as others start
when a ray of sun or the moon by night
busies itself about their room,
would she have been disturbed by the shape
in which an angel went;
she scarcely guessed that this sojourn
is irksome for angels. (O if we knew
how pure she was. Did not a hind, that,
recumbent, once espied her in the wood,
so lose itself in looking, that in it,
quite without pairing, the unicorn begot itself,
the creature of light, the pure creature—.)
Not that he entered, but that he,
the angel, so bent close to her
a youth's face that his gaze and that
with which she looked up struck together,
as though outside it were suddenly all empty
and what millions saw, did, bore,
were crowded into them: just she and he;
seeing and what is seen, eye and eye's delight
nowhere else save at this spot—: lo,
this is startling. And they were startled both.

Then the angel sang his melody.

𝕿𝖍𝖊 𝕬𝖓𝖌𝖊𝖑 𝕲𝖆𝖇𝖗𝖎𝖊𝖑

The carol "Gabriel's Message" (below) was originally written in Basque, or Euzkara, an ancient tongue still spoken in parts of northern Spain and southern France.

The an-gel Ga-bri-el from hea-ven came____, His wings as drifted snow, his eyes____ as flame; "All hail," said he, "thou low-ly maid-en Ma - ry____, Most high-ly fa-vored la - dy," Glo - - - - ri - a!

III
THE BLESSED BIRTH

AND IT CAME TO PASS IN THOSE days, that there went out a decree from Caesar Augustus, that all the world should be taxed. (And this taxing was first made when Cyrenius was governor of Syria.) And all went to be taxed, every one into his own city. And Joseph also went up from Galilee, out of the city of Nazareth, into Judaea, unto the city of David, which is called Bethlehem; (because he was of the house and lineage of David:) To be taxed with Mary his espoused wife, being great with child. And so it was, that, while they were there, the days were accomplished that she should be delivered. And she brought forth her firstborn son, and wrapped him in swaddling clothes, and laid him in a manger; because there was no room for them in the inn.

LUKE, 2:1-7

A LOVING MOTHER, *Mary attends to Jesus. This relief is at Chartres Cathedral, which was built to her glory in the 13th Century.*

BETHLEHEM'S HOUR
OF GLORY

GOD'S RADIANCE *pours down on the Nativity scene at Bethlehem in this delicate miniature from a 15th Century Book of Hours.*

A SIMPLE WOMAN goes on a journey with her husband and, while away from home, gives birth to a baby boy. This is the story, an ordinary story, that Luke sets forth in the plain verses on the preceding page. They tell of no miracles, make no demands on faith. And yet this birth is Christmas.

All the midnight masses, vesper services, clouds of drifting incense, choirs chanting in vaulted cathedrals, prayers arising from Christians of all persuasions and races on all the world's continents—all these celebrate Christmas. And so does all the bustling, warmhearted, pagan-tinged merriment: the gathering of the families, the decorating of the houses, the feasts and the gift-giving.

In the shadows, biding their time at this season of the year, stand those who would quarrel with Luke's account. They argue that Jesus was born at Nazareth, His parents' home, for there would be no reason for a tiring journey at this time.

The dissenters argue thus: Luke says—and no one questions—that

Jesus was born during Herod's reign. The saint further says that the reason for Mary and Joseph's journey to Bethlehem was to comply with an order by Cyrenius, the governor of Syria, to register for a census in the village of one's forebears. But, point out the dissidents, these two statements do not make sense: Herod died in 4 B.C. Thus, Jesus must have been born before then. Yet Cyrenius did not order the census until sometime between 6 and 9 A.D.

Luke altered fact, say skeptical scholars, to make Jesus' birth conform to the prophecy of Micah: " . . . thou, Bethlehem Ephratah . . . out of thee shall he come forth unto me that is to be ruler in Israel."

Yet other learned men agree with Luke. There is evidence, they suggest, that Cyrenius served two terms as governor and could well have presided over an earlier census—now forgotten—taken about 6 B.C., Jesus' probable birth year, during the final years of Herod's life.

Luke's account of the Birth is couched in the simplest of words: "And she brought forth her first-born son, and wrapped him in swaddling clothes, and laid him in a manger, because there was no room for them in the inn." Daniel-Rops, the eminent contemporary French writer, says in *Jesus and His Times,* "It is futile to attempt to embroider this plain statement." Yet the embroidery has gone on for centuries and still proceeds. The version which follows is almost pure speculation; no one can vouch for more than Luke reveals. Yet in their hearts, most Christians follow Mary and Joseph on their time-hallowed journey over the plains and hills.

In all probability, their route took them 90 miles from Nazareth to Jerusalem where, as reverent Jews,

they would have visited the Temple, then six miles more to Bethlehem. It would take the holy pair—Mary, perhaps 16 years old and approaching the end of her pregnancy, and Joseph, middle-aged, slow-moving and thoughtful—about four days to complete the trip, but every step of it must have been of absorbing interest.

Down the tortuous road the holy couple moved, jostled by Jewish traders, Nabataean caravaneers, Babylonian merchants with gold rings in their noses. Mary and Joseph passed by Jacob's well, where, one day, Jesus would converse with the Samaritan woman. Then they came in sight of Jerusalem, with the Temple, rebuilt by Herod after it was plundered by Crassus and Pompey, the Temple that stirred the heart of every Jew.

In truth it was a crowded, noisy city through which Mary and Joseph pushed to the Temple. Streets were narrow and houses often blocked the way. Above the hubbub came the roars of soldiers leading some poor wretch, his cross on his back, to his crucifixion. Mary, great with child, made her way past places her Son would consecrate in His agony —Gethsemane, Golgotha.

Then at Bethlehem, Luke states, there was no room for them in the inn, signifying, possibly, that they needed more privacy than the open court of an oriental hospice could give them. They went up to one of the hillside caves used by shepherds to shelter their animals, and there the Child was born. Mary and Joseph, soon joined by others, knelt to adore Him. And in adoration of a different kind, artists, each in the style of his own country and his own time, would paint and repaint that scene. Some of their worshipful creations appear on the following pages.

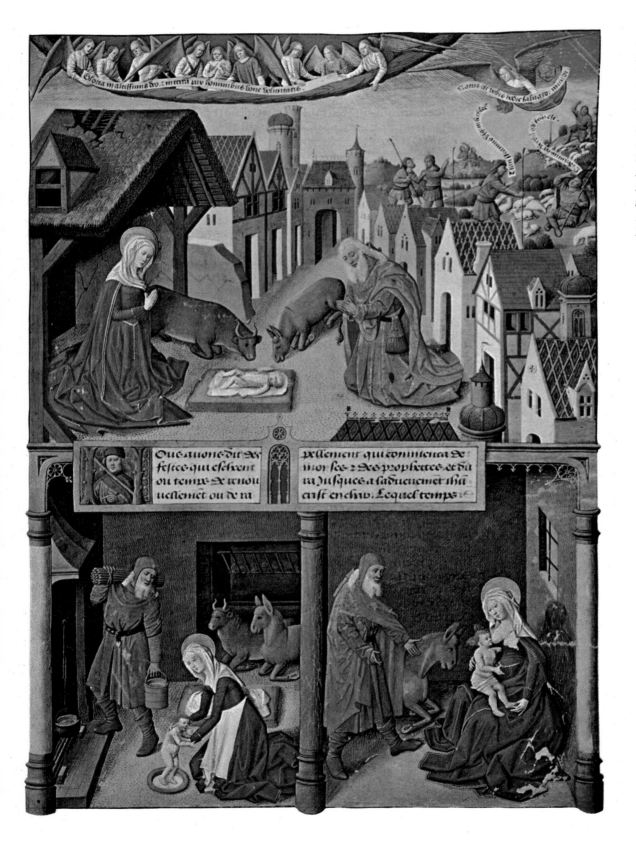

ADORATION of the Infant is presented in this unique view in a 15th Century manuscript illumination from "The Golden Legend" by Jacobus de Voragine. The Child, His parents, the ox and the ass are shown in a medieval European street, while in the fields outside the town the shepherds are shown approaching. Below are portrayed two tender and intimate scenes of Mary bathing and feeding the Babe as Joseph attends to chores.

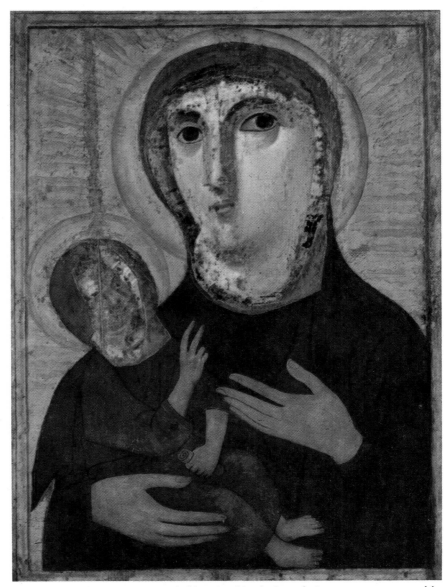

STERN AND ALOOF, *a Virgin, probably painted in the Seventh Century, gestures toward her Child. The picture, in Rome's Santa Maria Novella Church, was found under a later painting.*

MARY'S ALTERED ROLE IN CHRISTIANITY

After Mary had borne her Child, she wrapped Him in swaddling clothes and retired with Him to quiet places. We will see her again only fitfully: preparing her family for the flight into Egypt, worrying when the boy is lost in the Temple. She will be happy when He grants to her the miracle of the wine. She will understand when a voice from the crowd cries, "Blessed is the womb that bare thee and the paps which thou hast sucked," and He replies, "Yea rather, blessed are they that hear the word of God and keep it." She will stand and suffer by His Cross.

Once, in the joy of conception, she had sung "Yea, Behold, from henceforth all generations shall call me blessed." And this was so, although it was an austere blessedness, a cold and remote devotion that produced the Virgin in the picture above, sternly calling attention to the baby who is God. For this was the role the Church fathers first saw for her, a role of disciplinary firmness. It would take five centuries and the craving of generations for a merciful mediator at God's throne for mankind to recognize the Virgin's warmth and tenderness—qualities imbuing the statue opposite.

TENDER AND LOVING, *a Virgin and Child are sculpted in limestone over a door of Amiens Cathedral in France. Originally gilded, the statue now gleams goldenly in warm sunlight.*

37

THE INFANT MUSICIAN *is part of a complex representation of paradise by the 15th Century Master of the Upper Rhine. The walled garden is an old symbol of Mary's purity, derived from the "Song of Songs": "A garden inclosed is my sister, my spouse; a spring shut up, a fountain sealed."*

MOTHER OF MERCY AND HOPE

At services in all the great cathedrals, beloved hymns will resound again this Christmas season as they will in the village churches.

Carolers will softly sing, "Round yon Virgin mother and child, Holy Infant so tender and mild, sleep in heavenly peace." And many priests in ceremonial vestments will chant: "Mother of Jesus! Heaven's open gate, Star of the sea, support the fallen state of mortals, thou whose womb thy Maker bore; And yet, strange thing, a virgin, as before;

Who didst, from Gabriel's Hail, this news receive, Repenting sinners by thy prayers relieve."

For man, always a sinner, never felt his sinfulness more poignantly than he did in the Middle Ages. He felt that God was sublime, majestic, terrible, and there was no escaping from His stern justice, save perhaps through the intercession of a compassionate Mother.

The Middle Ages clung to her, and cathedral makers, sculptors, painters worked to her honor. Philoso-

phers sang her praises. Chaucer put Dante's words into his own tales: "Thow Mayde and Mooder, doghter of thy Sone Thow welle of mercy, synful soules cure."

Now the simple young woman of Nazareth was lost in the glittering world of art. With the Reformation, her exaltation diminished as many Protestant and Catholic theologians opposed elevating her to godhood. But already Mary had touched the depth of millions, and devotion to her became a never-ending well.

38

ENTHRONED IN A CHURCH, Mother and Child are depicted by Jan van Eyck in an architectural setting almost humorously remote from those in which Mary and Jesus lived their days.

AN AFRICAN MADONNA, *attending to her chores with her Child on her back, is the work of a pupil in a modern African school.*

THE VIRGIN IN ALL PARTS OF THE WORLD

With the passing centuries, devotion to the Blessed Virgin spread throughout the world. She became universal and varied. She was dark in Italy, fair-haired in Holland, thin in Spain and plump in France. In Mexico she was an Aztec maiden, the Virgin of Guadalupe, but she was also another, the Virgin of los Remedios, for the Spaniards; and in Warsaw she was a Polish woman. Chinese artists made her an almond-eyed lady in flowing robes and placed her in Chinese setting—a moon gate, a pagoda and a lantern festival. Maori artists dressed her in long grass skirts. African carvers made her a Negro and put heavy coils of beads around her neck; sometimes they showed her as a simple worker, worn yet full of happy courage. Indian artists made her a high-caste Hindu sitting serenely by a stream.

Princes and marshals placed nations and armies under her protection. Crusaders clanked off to the Holy Land shouting her praises, patriot warriors of Poland rallied to her banners and sometimes great hosts hurled themselves on one another, both of them roaring for victory in the name of the Virgin. At Guadalupe in Mexico, at Lourdes in France, Fatima in Portugal and in other places, she is said to have appeared to mankind. And to the shrines in those places, the poor and sick and pious come to pray for her aid even today.

A NEW MEXICAN MADONNA *holding her Child dates from the 19th Century. Their attire and skin tones suggest Indian influences.*

A CHINESE NATIVITY *is shown in a painting by Lu Hung Hien, who in 1941 was a student at the Catholic University of Peking. Missionaries were in China as early as the Seventh Century, but it was not until the period between the two world wars that a Chinese school of Christian art, hauntingly delicate and filled with a brooding peace, arose—and all too briefly flourished.*

FRANCIS' HOLY CUSTOM

At Greccio, Italy, in 1223, St. Francis of Assisi re-created the birth of Christ using life-size scenery, live actors, a wax figure of the Babe and living animals. Ever since, the crèche, or crib, has been a Christmas tradition. Sculptors, architects and painters have helped construct crèches, and

those built in such cities as Munich and Barcelona are noted for their ornate handiwork. But few equal the elaborateness of the one above, built for King Charles III of Naples in the 18th Century. Around Mary, Joseph and the Child clusters a busy Neapolitan world. While dining at an inn, a family on pilgrimage listens to a band. Porters lug the heavy trunks of the Magi, and over everyone hover cupids and elegant angels.

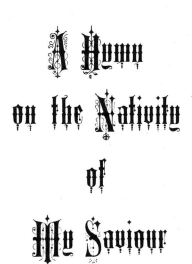

A Hymn on the Nativity of My Saviour

Ben Jonson, Elizabethan playwright (1572-1637), is firmly associated with Christmas chiefly because of the plays he wrote for court festivities. Here is his description of mankind's universal joy at the miracle of the Nativity.

I sing the birth was born to-night,
The Author both of life and light;
   The angels so did sound it,
And like the ravished shepherds said,
Who saw the light, and were afraid,
   Yet searched, and true they found it.

The Son of God, th' Eternal King,
That did us all salvation bring,
   And freed the soul from danger;
He whom the whole world could not take,
The Word, which heaven and earth did make;
   Was now laid in a manger.

The Father's wisdom willed it so,
The Son's obedience knew no No,
   Both wills were in one stature;
And as that wisdom had decreed,
The Word was now made Flesh indeed,
   And took on Him our nature.

What comfort by Him do we win,
Who made Himself the price of sin,
   To make us heirs of glory!
To see this Babe, all innocence,
A martyr born in our defence;
   Can man forget this story?

Joseph's Vision

Few versions of the Nativity story pay more than passing attention to Joseph. An exception is the Book of James, or Protevangelium, one of the New Testament apocryphal texts. In it appears this fragment, ostensibly in Joseph's words.

And I Joseph walked, and I walked not; and I looked up into the air, and saw the air violently agitated; and I looked up at the pole of heaven, and saw it stationary, and the fowls of heaven still; and I looked at the earth and saw a vessel lying, and workmen reclining by it, and their hands in the vessel, and those who handled did not handle it, and those who took did not lift, and those who presented it to their mouth did not present it, but the faces of all were looking up; and I saw the sheep scattered, and the sheep stood, and the shepherd lifted up his hand to strike them, and his hand remained up; and I looked at the stream of the river, and I saw that the mouths of the kids were down, and not drinking; and everything which was being impelled forward was intercepted in its course.

A Gothic Noel

Of the many elaborations on the Nativity story, few offer the blend of reverence, humor and imagination found in the tale condensed here. Written by Jehan Le Povremoyne, a contemporary French journalist and lecturer, it has been translated and adapted by Audrey Foote.

High above the drowsing village stands the Gothic cathedral, its spires pointing to the heavens. In the belltowers the wind murmurs an ancient and plaintive refrain as it did once upon a time over the stable of Bethlehem. The village, at peace beneath a clear night sky and the glittering stars, snuggles against its hillsides and goes to sleep.

At the cathedral, only St. Benoit is awake. He watches the lights die out in the twisted alleys where the antique signboards sway in the wind. He listens to the diminishing sounds of life in the town and the vanishing footsteps of vagrants returning from the taverns. And then, sure of not being seen by any human being, St. Benoit steps out of his niche by the grand portal and climbs the façade of the cathedral, hand over hand clinging to the rooted vines, until he reaches the tympan over the main doorway, where stand the sculptured figures of the Biblical prophets and martyrs.

"Noah? Isaiah? Abraham?"

He calls out, tugs at the hem of a mantle and with his stick prods the sleeping ones.

"Noah, it is I, Benoit, Brother Benoit."

"Brother Benoit?"

"Yes, from down below, from beside the little doorway."

"Ah yes; well, what do you wish, my brother?"

"I wanted to tell you, Noah, it is the eve of Noel. Noel, the feast of the redemption. The glorious Nativity on earth of the son of God. Noah?"

The mumble of his voice in his white beard is like a breeze in the forest of Ile de France. Amid the sculptured leaves and branches, allelulias seem to echo.

"Yes, Benoit," Noah answers, "I understand. I know. Let us give praise."

"No, not yet. Since Easter of the year 1426, I have been thinking over an idea which I wanted to confide to you. Tell me what you think of it."

And in the ear of Noah—an ear grey with ancient dust—St. Benoit confesses his great project. It must be something magnificent, fantastic, celestial and pious all at once; Noah, gay as the time he drank too much wine, kisses St. Benoit on both stony cheeks, cheeks eroded by the tears of the rain. At the tympan of the Old Testament they awaken the statues; the whole bizarre throng of Genesis, from Adam to Nathanael, arises.

And now they make their way along the exterior of the cathedral, along the balconies, under the flying buttresses; from time to time they pause and gaze down from the parapets on the sleeping village below. A rising murmur fills the towers, the spires, and vibrates against the stone roses from which the petals fall soundlessly on the parvis; the light folds of the virgins' draperies flutter.

"What is it?" all the Biblical figures whisper. "Why are you awakening us?"

All the saints of the New Testament now, the great saints from St. Martin to St. Louis, from the apostles to the most humble monks, have stepped out from their places. They are all different, no one is of the same size or height . . . there are large ones, lean in their long straight robes, little ones in their mantles and hoods. Some wear crowns, some miters . . . some are barefoot, others shod in the finest sandals; but they are all very old, very good, very holy—and very beautiful with all the beauty of Gothic sculpture.

And amid all this, St. Benoit continues to preach.

"My brothers, we are here to find the Holy Mother of God. So be it."

"So be it," they all mumble after him. "But what do you think of this, Chrysostome? A pretty sermon, but Benoit is making fun of us. Why does he waken us like this after so many centuries?"

But St. Benoit does not let himself be intimidated by either the kings or the people—far less by the clergy. Undaunted, he leads the crowd of saints toward the apse. For it is at the apse, high on the gable as on the prow of a ship, that the figure of the Virgin Mary stands, Our Lady of the Waves, for the protection of mariners. The saints press forward along the balconies, perch on the arches and on the lead roof; then from the throng arises an exquisite prayer towards the Madonna. Her hands joined, her head crowned, she steps forth from among the stars which sprinkle the velvety drapery of the sky; she listens to them and then smiles.

"Merciful Virgin, beautiful madonna," St. Benoit chants as the others chorus behind him.

"Queen! Queen of the angels!" the cherubs shout enthusiastically. . . .

St. Benoit speaks:

"Hail, Mary, full of grace. But the Saviour is not with you, and it is the eve of Noel. My brothers and I—we would be so happy if you would—"

"That Benoit, would you believe it," mutters St. Onesiphore. "What audacity!"

"If you would, Holy Mother, relive among us the fete of the Nativity."

A great silence falls on the cathedral; all are silent, holding their breath, listening.

"Relive the Nativity."

And in answer the Virgin steps down from her flowered pedestal. But St. Benoit stops her as she places one foot on the gutter. He is in command.

"This must be done properly," he says. "You must not go on foot, my lady, we—"

"We will carry you," volunteer the tiny angels who have but the tips of wings on their shoulders.

"Angels! will you do me the kindness of going off to play elsewhere? And just as fast as you can." St. Benoit climbs up on a broken buttress and then orders: "This way, Old Testament. All the Old Testament, by hierarchic order, naturally. But of course, Adam and Eve first. Please let them move up to the head of the line—the kings next. Then the prophets—hurry up, kings, will you please hurry up. There now, all the Old Testament marches in front. Yes, the angels can play their trumpets—but not too loudly! Don't play *yet*, angels! Wait a minute! O Holy Mother, what a lot of trouble!"

"Perhaps you would like your friends near you?" simpers St. Pacome.

"My friend," the Virgin says, "I wish only Joseph near to me—"

"Oh, St. Joseph!" exclaims St. Benoit. "I forgot all about St. Joseph! Where are you, Joseph? Joseph?"

The crowd of statues turns in search of the blessed carpenter. He is not to be found.

"St. Exupère, would you go and look for St. Joseph? Tell him that Madame the Virgin asks for him." St. Exupère and his cohorts go off.

"The New Testament will follow after Our Mother," Benoit commands. "The apostles first, yes, the apostles. St. Peter, stand there please, beside your brother. St. Paul—ah, but St. Paul, still preaching? You set a bad example! But no, look now, after the apostles come the martyrs. The popes? The popes? Will you Holinesses, please be more cooperative! After the monks—yes, *after* them."

At this moment there is a stir in the crowd and St. Exupère emerges.

"Here is Joseph, long live St. Joseph," shout the saints. "Where was he?"

"Joseph thinks of everything. While we were here fussing futilely, he went to find the only mount which God has glorified on this earth—for the services which he rendered to the Mother and the Son. St. Joseph went to find—"

And the poor man of Nazareth steps aside; there stands a donkey. Alas, a very little donkey, from the tympan of the flight into Egypt; skinny, low slung, and missing ears and tail.

The Virgin smiles at her husband and then at the beast. With her beautiful fine hand of white stone, Our Lady strokes the worn little back; it is still solid enough in its carving, however, to carry the Madonna. And then with infinite precaution, for Mary suddenly feels herself heavy as on the day she left Nazareth, the maidens help her mount the blessed donkey.

St. Benoit, hoarse with emotion, announces:

"On route for the procession of Noel!"

Across the roofs of the old Gothic cathedral, among the marvelous stone lilies and vines, among the treasures worked by men who were artists and artists who were saints, the wonderful and droll procession of statues advances.

See them pass . . . across the luxuriant flora of stone flowers and rose windows and arabesques . . . down the stairways of the towers, advancing onto the large square before the cathedral where not even a dog scampers. The nave is soon filled, then the transepts, even the rood loft. The Virgin meanwhile has reached the chapel in the apse, *her* chapel.

On the steps of the high altar the Virgin reposes. Joseph, leaning on his staff, contemplates her, half smiling, half sad. To one side the little donkey kneels, and at the other an ox from the niche of St. Matthew, and all gaze upon the open space of blue and gold carpet where Jesus is to be born.

The throng of saints presses close to the screen of the choir which the beloved St. John has closed about his mother. The Old Testament and the New Testament await the Nativity. But just then St. Francis in his cowl approaches St. Benoit.

"My brother Benoit," he says. "It is not only mankind who should witness the Birth of Our Saviour. Our brothers the beasts would rejoice around the Virgin—"

And the Franciscans leave the cathedral, climb once more the pillars and the lintels, up to the highest and most hidden corners, and coax forth the fantastic fauna of the Middle Ages: horses, goats, hippocamps, crabs, scorpions, bulls and the beasts of the Apocalypse, all chiseled with love in the ateliers of the time of St. Louis. The animals descend, tumbling and leaping and cavorting, and under the guidance of the little Brothers, take their places in the majestic nave of the cathedral. The whole of the animal creation is there beside the ox and ass of Bethlehem: sheep, quail, piglets, lions, eagles and all the birds of the islands and the heavens, and all the fish of the oceans and all the creatures of the Gothic imagination.

All the sculptures of the cathedral are there, but alas, the Divine Infant does not descend. The angels sing in vain, St. Joseph struggles against drowsiness, the little donkey has cramps in his knees; all the little animals disport themselves like acrobats to divert the mother of God—but Jesus is not reborn.

But where is St. Benoit?

"Benoit? Benoit?" the saints whisper.

Benoit breaks through the crowd. Having put aside his cross and miter of abbé, Benoit lifts up on a fine folded cloth a beautiful smiling child, all glorious, with a globe of the world in one hand

and a royal crown on his brow. On both knees before the Virgin, Benoit speaks:

"Woman. Woman. Here is your son."

The saints are ecstatic, the apse glorious with supernatural light; the little animals twitter with ineffable joy in the torrent of grace, the Paradise, which descends upon them.

But suddenly a volley of bells shakes the cathedral. From the high belfries glistening in the dawn comes the rumble of the huge bells, howling like

the ocean, into the overturned vessel where the saints of stone are praying.

"The angelus! The angelus!"

And the statues are immediately again on the roofs, the galleries, the towers, the tympans and the pillars, in their places of worldly immobility; and their escapade of an eve of Noel would never have been known to man had the poet not read in their ecstatic eyes the miraculous vision of which they dream now until the end of time.

The Rocking Carol

Lullabies sung to the heavenly baby—they are called "berceuses" in France and "Wiegenlieder" in Germany—send many an ordinary baby to sleep. The one below comes from an 18th Century Czech song, "Hajej, nynej, Ježíšku."

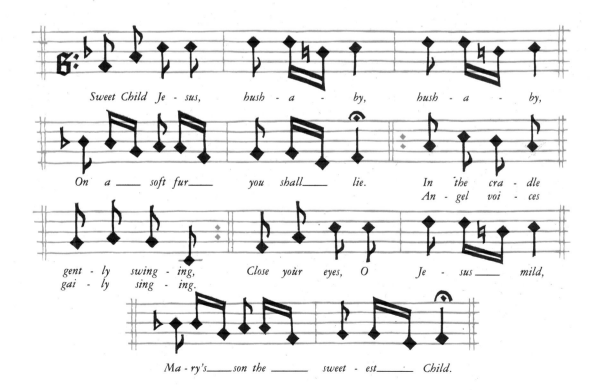

Sweet Child Je - sus, hush - a - by, hush - a - by,

On a ___ soft fur ___ you shall ___ lie. In the cra - dle
An - gel voi - ces

gent - ly swing - ing, Close your eyes, O Je - sus ___ mild,
gai - ly sing - ing.

Ma - ry's ___ son the ___ sweet - est ___ Child.

IV

THE COURIERS OF GOD

AND THERE WERE IN THE SAME country shepherds abiding in the field, keeping watch over their flock by night. And, lo, the angel of the Lord came upon them, and the glory of the Lord shone round about them: and they were sore afraid. And the angel said unto them, Fear not: for, behold, I bring you good tidings of great joy, which shall be to all people. For unto you is born this day in the city of David a Saviour, which is Christ the Lord. And this shall be a sign unto you; Ye shall find the babe wrapped in swaddling clothes, lying in a manger. And suddenly there was with the angel a multitude of the heavenly host praising God, and saying, Glory to God in the highest, and on earth peace, good will toward men.

LUKE, 2:8-14

FROM THE REALMS OF GLORY *angels come to worship the Child. This is a detail from a Gozzoli fresco in Florence's Medici Palace.*

EXALTED
CHOIR
IN
SONGS OF PRAISE

PLAYING A LUTE, *an angel rejoices at Jesus' birth. The figure illuminates a decorative border in a medieval devotional book.*

NO FIGURES in the Christmas story are more delightful than the heavenly host of angels. Wise in their knowledge of God's ways, childlike in their direct speech and action, they burst upon the momentous events with a joy and a consideration for man that at once brings God closer to the simplest shepherds and emphasizes His awesome power and majesty. Glorifying God in heaven and offering peace and good will to men, the angels bring a touch of the divine to all who hear their message.

Angels appear suddenly and they act purposefully. For angels have a special role in the Bible that requires them to leave their place in God's firmament and to associate with His people on earth. Throughout the Old and New Testaments, the angels appear to man as messengers of God.

They bring comfort, as in Genesis when an angel advises the Egyptian maid Hagar that, if she returns to Abram and Sarai, her seed will multiply so that "it shall not be numbered for multitude."

Angels bring warnings, as when they announce to Lot the imminent destruction of Sodom and tell him to flee with his wife and daughters.

They bring tests of belief, as when Satan inflicts disease and death upon Job in a trial of his faith in God.

And they bring deliverance, too, as when Daniel says after a night in the lions' den that it was an angel who "hath shut the lions' mouths, that they have not hurt me."

Angels deliver perhaps the two most important messages in the life of Jesus. It is Gabriel who tells Mary that she shall bring forth a son of whose kingdom "there shall be no end." And it is also an angel, whose "countenance was like lightning," who rolls back the stone at the sepulcher and gives those who have come to mourn Jesus the message: "He is not here: for He is risen."

From these and other references, theologians have worked out an elaborate—but not always consistent—structure of the hierarchy and duties of the angels. They are ranked in this descending order of sublimity: seraphim, cherubim, thrones, dominions, virtues, powers, principalities, archangels and angels. Only archangels and angels, the two lowest orders, appear to man. Of these, the only ones to become known by name to man are the four archangels who, Hebrew tradition says, sustain the throne of god.

They are: Michael, captain general of the hosts of heaven in eternal combat with the Prince of Hell, who will sound his trumpet to awaken the dead for the Last Judgment; Gabriel, bearer of good news, who not only announced the coming of Jesus to Mary, but also told Daniel of the return of the Jews from captivity, and Zacharias that his wife Elizabeth would bear a son who would become John the Baptist; Raphael, chief of the guardian angels, who, tradition holds, brought the tidings of Christ's birth to the shepherds; and Uriel, who, as Christ's ambassador, appeared to the Apostles at Emmaus after His death. The duties of the others appear to be in heaven, guarding the throne of God, praising Him, doing His bidding and guarding men on earth.

The role of the guardian angels is illustrated by Jesus in Matthew 18:10 when He says of children: "Take heed that ye despise not one of these little ones; for I say unto you, that in heaven their angels do always behold the face of my Father...."

Angels have been favorites of such poets as Milton and of painters, though at first the Church forbade their representation. In the early Renaissance, artists usually depicted angels as severe-looking men with wings. Gradually, their features softened and they became boys with curling hair. Later, as in the Piero della Francesca at the right and the Fra Angelico *(following pages),* they became quite feminine in appearance.

Angels have long been associated with music; to medieval scholastics and artists it seemed only natural that the angelic host should, by singing and playing, imitate the perfect harmony of heaven. And through the ages composers have set the angels' words to music.

Belief in angels is a matter of individual faith among Protestants. It is an article of faith in Roman Catholicism. Angels generally are described as having been created by God on a level that places them above man but beneath God himself. Satan was an angel of God until he fell. With him fell other angels, who became demons. Theologians disagree on whether they fell because of pride or because of jealousy of mankind. The question also arises whether Satan does the bidding of God, as when he gets the Lord's permission to tempt Job, or whether he is a being independent from and opposed to God.

STRUMMING RENAISSANCE LUTES, *angels sing at the Nativity in this late 15th Century work by Piero della Francesca. In this detail, Piero tried to suppress otherworldly elements; he omitted the angels' wings and halos. As heavenly beings, supernatural in freedom of spirit and ability to appear and disappear instantly on God's errands, angels are usually shown winged.*

THREE ANGEL MUSICIANS, *from a grouping of 12 by Fra Angelico, use medieval instruments to praise the Virgin and Child.*

AN ANGELIC
ENSEMBLE
IN
PRAISE TO GOD

In modern folklore, angels seem to play the harp almost to the exclusion of other musical instruments. But medieval painters and sculptors heard the music of the heavenly heralds in a different way. When de-picting angels, the artists furnished them with instruments of the artists' own time. In the examples on these and the following pages, the angel musicians are playing instruments well known in the 15th Century, yet not unlike many still in use today.

When he painted his triptych for the Linen Guild of Florence, Fra Angelico included an arch of 12 angels surrounding the Madonna and Child and praising them with an ensem-

ble that presages many modern musical instruments. Three of the celestial members of Fra Angelico's grouping are shown above. The instruments they play are, from the left: a *vièle*, an ancestor of all modern bowed string instruments; a psaltery, an early relative of the zither and of many other plucked instruments; and a tambourine, unchanged today and still familiar in orchestral percussion sections.

REJOICING ANGELS *attend Mary in a section of a carved wood altarpiece representing incidents from the Virgin's life (next pages). Carved by the Master Arnt between 1483 and 1492, it is installed in the Church of St. Nicholas in Calcar, Germany. The angels are playing medieval instruments.*

WHY ANGELS HAVE WINGS

Since the Bible gives few precise physical descriptions of angels, their appearance has been individually interpreted by artists and writers. The modern Christian, however, has a definite picture of angels fixed in his mind. How this image developed is traced by classicist Gilbert Highet in his article "An Iconography of Heavenly Beings," which is excerpted below.

HOW
IS IT, THEN,
THAT whenever we hear the word "angel," we see a being with large wings? How is it that the image in our minds is a graceful shape with flowing robes and floating hair and kindly gaze, sexless or almost sexless, or perhaps with a hint of the feminine? God's messenger Gabriel, who spoke so authoritatively to Zacharias and Mary, was evidently masculine in form and nature. But painters have often depicted the angel of the Annunciation as a gentle visitor, like a maid of honor sent to pay homage to a princess; and the angel does not "come in" to Mary's room but flies down from heaven on a pair of birdlike wings.

This is because Christian art is a blend of Jewish mysticism and Greek imagery. The Jews, for whom the Old Testament and much of the New Testament were written, thought of God as being free of all bodily form and his messengers as human in appearance—mediums or diplomats, as it were, characterless save for their mission. But the Greeks, or at least the Greek artists and poets, could not think of the divine as formless, with no resemblance to humanity. To them, a god wore the shape of a perfect man or woman, endowed with superhuman powers. And the messenger of divinity must surely have the appurtenances of swift and graceful flight. Therefore Christian artists,

working in the Graeco-Roman tradition, gave their angels the wings of Victory and Eros and the Genius. But this did not happen all at once. Before the change was made, there was a long period of doubt and resistance. When the change did come, it was part of the great conversion of the pagan world.

THE
EARLIEST
CHRISTIAN artists portray Jesus neither as an individual with distinctive features nor as a rabbi. Instead, they show him as one of the symbolic figures established by the vivid Greek imagination: Orpheus, teacher and poet, Hermes the friendly deity, carrying a lamb on his shoulders. In the same way, during the first four Christian centuries, angels are not shown as having wings. They are (as in the Scriptures) handsome youths, beardless, wearing ordinary clothes (ankle-length gown and cloak), standing or moving humanly upon the ground. But this was scarcely satisfactory. Artists wanted to distinguish the heavenly messengers from other young male figures such as the disciples of Jesus and Jesus himself. Greek and Roman Christian poets, elaborating on the Gospel stories, introduced traditional classical imagery. Thus, the good Paulinus of Nola, after describing the angel Gabriel's visit to Zacharias, concludes with something which is not in the Scriptures: "He spoke, and glided on wings into thin air." Mystics and divines reflected on the strange powers given by the Almighty to his envoys—their sudden appearances and disappearances, their rapid movement, their ubiquity—and concluded that, although human in form, they must be superhuman both in their beauty and in their power of flight.

ABOUT
A. D.
400, after long suspense and mounting pressure, an ancient and enormous dam broke. The waters of the Christian spirit gushed into dry pagan channels, filling them with new energy and reviving much of the moribund life along their banks. Again and again, then and thereafter, we see pagan philosophical ideas, aesthetic patterns, imaginative symbols, and social and religious customs taken over by Christianity, rededicated and, without destruction, transformed. One of the oldest houses of worship in existence is the cathedral of Syracuse. It is simply the temple of Athena, built five centuries before Christ, and after twelve hundred years of paganism, converted into a Christian church. In the same way, the angels of Jewish

and Christian Scripture took on the wings, the grace, and the spiritual intensity of Graeco-Roman spirits and demigods.

In Greek and Roman belief, an unseen guardian accompanies each of us from birth to death and (as Menander says) "initiates us into the mystic rites of life." He is our daemon, or our Genius. On sculptured tombs, the Genius sometimes appears at the moment of death, extinguishing his torch or, as the soul, flying away from the funeral pyre into heaven. This kindly companion gave his wings and something of his personality to the Christian angels.

THE IMAGE
OF
VICTORY

had always accompanied the Roman emperors. When they, too, became Christians, she did not leave them. In the imperial palace at Constantinople the emperor's throne was flanked by two Victories with outspread wings, each holding a laurel crown. In Christian churches, too, the winged Victories now appeared, carrying the palms of triumph—as they did for Greek athletes at the great games, as the Jews did when they greeted Christ at his entry into Jerusalem, and as the blessed do standing before the throne of God in the Revelation of Saint John. In one strange, mystical picture from northern Italy, we see a procession centering on a winged female figure who stands beside a basket of bread and a cup of wine. The spirit is Victory, the bread and wine symbolize Jesus; and the two together mean *Christos Nika*, "Christ is Victorious!"

So it is that just as Greek and Roman temples became Christian houses of worship, just as subtle Greek philosophical thought and strong Roman organizing power were transfused into the Church, just as the wealth and vigor of Greek rhetoric and Roman poetry were put to the service of the new religion, so the messengers, the guardians, and the heavenly visitors of Graeco-Roman paganism gave their flight, their dignity, and their charm to the angels of Christian art and literature.

A PAPAL INTERPRETATION

Pope Pius XII (1876-1958) chose as his papal name the very quality for which he was most venerated by Roman Catholics. Once, addressing pilgrims from America, he again revealed his piety in these words about the guardian angels.

No one is so humble, but he has angels to attend him. So glorious, so pure, so wonderful they are, and yet they are given to be your fellow-wayfarers, charged to watch carefully over you, lest you fall away from Christ, their Lord. Not only they wish to defend you against dangers lurking along the way; they are also active at your side with a word of encouragement to your souls, as you strive to ascend higher and higher to closeness to God through Christ.

CHRISTMAS EVE

Angel voices mingle with Christmas bells in this thoughtful work by Robert Bridges (1844-1930), England's Poet Laureate for 17 years.

A Frosty Christmas-eve ' when the stars were shining
Fared I forth alone ' where westward falls the hill
And from many a village ' in the water'd valley
Distant music reached me ' peals of bells a-ringing:
The constellated sounds ' ran sprinkling on earth's floor
As the dark vault above ' with stars was spangled o'er.

Then sped my thought to keep ' that first Christmas of all
When the shepherds watching ' by their folds ere the dawn
Heard music in the fields ' and marvelling could not tell
Whether it were angels ' or the bright stars singing.

Now blessed be the towers ' that crown England so fair
That stand up strong in prayer ' unto God for our souls:
Blessed be their founders ' (said I) and our country-folk
Who are ringing for Christ ' in the belfries tonight
With arms lifted to clutch ' the rattling ropes that race
Into the dark above ' and the mad romping din.

But to me heard afar ' it was heav'nly music
Angels' song comforting ' as the comfort of Christ
When he spake tenderly ' to his sorrowful flock:
The old words came to me ' by the riches of time
Mellow'd and transfigured ' as I stood on the hill
Hark'ning in the aspect ' of th' eternal silence.

CARE IN HEAVEN?

It was a belief of the Renaissance that angels played a vigorous role in the affairs of man. It was in this context that Edmund Spenser (1552-1599) wrote, in his great epic "The Faerie Queene," these two stanzas in praise of angels.

And is there care in heaven? and is there love
In heavenly spirits to these creatures bace,
That may compassion of their evilles move?
There is: else much more wretched were the cace
Of men then beasts. But O! th' exceeding grace
Of highest God that loves his creatures so,
And all his workes with mercy doth embrace,
That blessed Angels he sends to and fro,
To serve to wicked man, to serve his wicked foe.

How oft do they their silver bowers leave,
To come to succour us that succour want!
How oft do they with golden pineons cleave
The flitting skyes, like flying Pursuivant,
Against fowle feendes to ayd us millitant!
They for us fight, they watch and dewly ward,
And their bright Squadrons round about us plant;
And all for love, and nothing for reward.
O! why should hevenly God to men have such regard?

A CLOUD OF ANGELS

The distinguished American Quaker leader Rufus M. Jones (1863-1948) once journeyed to Bethlehem for Christmas. His mystical experience there, which he describes in the extract from "The Shepherd Who Missed the Manger," attests to the Holy Land's ageless inspiration.

We sat under rustling olive trees and watched the sun sink over the Plains of Sharon and seem to fall into the Mediterranean beyond. Before sunset we had noticed strange masses of thin fleecy clouds, covering the sky, with areas of blue separating the clouds. But we thought nothing of it—they were just clouds, such as we have in America. But all of a sudden as the sun went out of sight these fleecy

clouds began to turn red. In a little while the entire sky from the Mount of Olives in the East to the Great Sea in the West was filled with what looked like Seraphim, with outspread wings; for as everybody knows, I hope, the Seraphim, which are the highest order of angelic beings, are red—burning with love. And in between the red Seraphim were blue spaces which it was easy to imagine were Cherubim, for, as everybody knows, I am sure, Cherubim are always blue, and are the supreme knowers, "the great Intelligences," beholding the truth with their minds. Here just above our heads, on the Shepherds' Field, on Christmas Eve, was a sky full of what looked to us like Seraphim and Cherubim. We beheld it with awe and wonder, and though we heard no words from above, we said in our hearts "Glory to God in the highest." And under the spell of what we had seen, we silently climbed the hill to hear the midnight Christmas Service in the Church of the Nativity. Perhaps not twice in a thousand years would there come a sky like that—and we were there the night it came! I have forgotten the service that followed, but the memory of the sky full of Seraphim and Cherubim over the Shepherds' Field has never quite faded out of mind.

Within the Frame

In the popular imagination, angels changed slowly from grand figures to sentimentalized children. Kenneth Grahame (1859-1931), the author of the beloved children's story "The Wind in the Willows," was a boy when he and his brothers and sisters saw their first picture of classical angels. Grahame describes the episode in this excerpt from "Dream Days."

This left two or three more angels, who peeped or perched behind the main figures with a certain subdued drollery in their faces, as if the thing had gone on long enough, and it was now time to upset something or kick up a row of some sort. We knew these good folk to be saints and angels, because we had been told they were; otherwise we should never have guessed it. Angels, as we knew them in our Sunday books, were vapid, colourless, uninteresting characters, with straight up-and-down sort of figures, white nightgowns, white wings, and the same straight yellow hair parted in the middle. They were serious, even melancholy; and we had no desire to have any traffic with them. These bright bejewelled little persons, however, piquant of face and radiant of feather, were evidently hatched from quite a different egg, and we felt we might have interests in common with them. Short-nosed, shock-headed, with mouths that went up at the corners and with an evident disregard for all their fine clothes, they would be the best of good company, we felt sure, if only we could manage to get at them. One doubt alone disturbed my mind. In games requiring agility, those wings of theirs would give them a tremendous pull. Could they be trusted to play fair? I asked Selina, who replied scornfully that angels *always* played fair.

Angels We Have Heard on High

According to Luke, the angels said "Glory to God in the highest." Tradition insists they sang it, but angels' talk could well sound like song to man. In the French carol below, which celebrates the angelic message, their words appear in the chorus, which is sung in Latin.

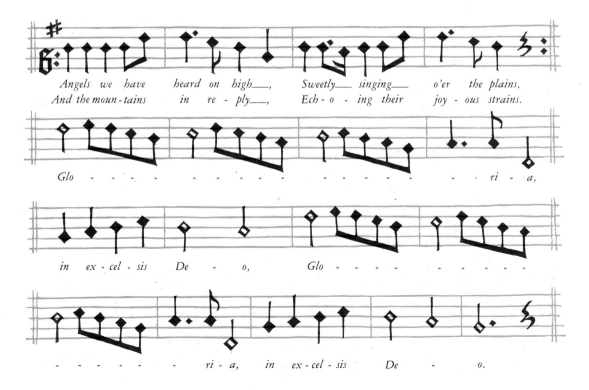

Angels we have heard on high___, Sweetly___ singing___ o'er the plains,
And the moun-tains in re-ply___, Ech-o-ing their joy-ous strains.

Glo - - - - - - - - - - - - - - - ri - a,

in ex-cel-sis De - o, Glo - - - - - - - -

- - - - - ri - a, in ex-cel-sis De - o.

V

THE FIRST WITNESSES

AND IT CAME TO PASS, AS THE angels were gone away from them into heaven, the shepherds said one to another, Let us now go even unto Bethlehem, and see this thing which is come to pass, which the Lord hath made known unto us. And they came with haste, and found Mary, and Joseph, and the babe lying in a manger. And when they had seen it, they made known abroad the saying which was told them concerning this child. And all they that heard it wondered at those things which were told them by the shepherds.... And the shepherds returned, glorifying and praising God for all the things that they had heard and seen, as it was told unto them.

LUKE, 2:15-18, 20

GRIZZLED SHEPHERDS *receive the news of Jesus' birth from an angel in this painting by an unknown master of the 15th Century.*

LIFE
OF HARDSHIP
AND LOVE
OF THE FLOCK

IN A SHEPHERDS' FIELD, *a green-winged angel announces Jesus' birth. This vivid miniature was painted in the 15th Century.*

THE FIRST MEN to see and worship Jesus were shepherds. They were tending their sheep when the angel appeared in the night sky and told them the good news of His birth. "With haste" they led their flocks toward Bethlehem.

The winter rainy season had begun and the steep Judean hills streamed with rain. Nights were cold and there was often frost on the ground. When they could, the shepherds penned their flocks—goats intermingled with the sheep—in caves for the night, and when there were no caves they sheltered their sheep under trees and took refuge themselves in tents woven from goat hair. When they arrived in Bethlehem they could, they knew, pen their flocks in the natural caves in the hills outside the town.

They were rough and simple men —*am ha'aretz*, the common people —and they were armed against the dangers of their work. They carried weapons: a knife, a sling, a cudgel and a staff. Their clothes were those of the poor: a knee-length tunic, a sleeved jacket, and a coat made of sheepskin, tanned with the wool still on.

They were despised by the Sadducees for their poverty and dis-

trusted by the Pharisees for their careless observance of the law. Yet they were the first to worship the Child. They knelt and perhaps offered such gifts as they had: a cruse of oil, a piece of cheese, a fleece for a blanket.

They had little to give. Their life was frugal. They could take few stores on their long wanderings. At streams they caught fish and on the hills they snared birds. Fat from the sheep's tail, mixed with pellets of lean, was the only meat they carried with them. They carried a pouch of dough and made a crude bread by slapping the dough onto hot stones. They ate, if they were few, from one dish, scooping up food with wedges of bread. In spring and summer the ewes provided them with milk, butter and cheese. In spring, too, with the hard rains over and the pastures green, flocks fed easily again.

Spring was the start of the shepherd's year. In March and April the ewes, which had been bred five months before, lambed. The flock was shorn in May. Shearing was a festival time. After the sheep had been dipped in pools, and clipped, and then dipped again, the shepherds who had gathered at the pools celebrated with prayers, dances and songs. It was their harvesttime.

Then they moved northward into the hills until the hot winds dried up the hill fodder, forcing the flocks into the valleys below. Often, by autumn, the land was stripped bare. When the sheep had only thorns for food, the shepherd often brought them to carob trees, whose pods they ate, or to sycamores, whose fruit grew in clusters like figs.

Shepherds, in those days, led their sheep, they did not drive them. And each ram, ewe and lamb had a name.

When the shepherd called, the sheep came to his side. The shepherd led because, although he had dogs, his dogs did not muster the flock. They were guards. Shaggy and fierce, they fought off foxes, jackals and even wolves. Also, leading, the shepherd could guide his sheep away from grain fields where the flock would destroy the crop, or avoid fields in which weeds grew that could poison his sheep. With his staff he killed snakes in the way and with his sling he frightened off hawks.

To guide his flock, the shepherd needed to know the terrain in every detail—where the pasturage was good, where he could ford a river, where there were pure springs. And to keep the flock moving, he would have to carry a lamb if it were lame. "He shall feed his flock like a shepherd," Isaiah had said of the Messiah in his prophecy, "he shall gather the lambs with his arm, and carry them in his bosom, and shall gently lead those that are with young."

So it was fitting that the first witnesses of the birth of Jesus were shepherds, called up from their field where they sat by the fire.

In the pages which follow, these men of humble birth are shown in paintings, woodcuts and miniatures as medieval and earlier artists saw them. In each work these simple shepherds seem to know that their lowly station will be of no hindrance at Bethlehem, that they will be as welcome as the Kings who will come later. They appear to know that the Child whom they have been invited to see and to worship, the Child whom later generations would call "the good shepherd," would one day declare: "Whosoever therefore shall humble himself . . . the same is greatest in the kingdom of heaven."

WARMING THEIR HANDS, *two shepherds keep watch over their flock, penned for the night. An imaginary landscape of Bethlehem rises behind them. Sano di Pietro, the 15th Century Sienese artist who painted this scene, combined roughhewn realism with a deep sense of awe. The shepherds, sitting with their eyes upraised, seem ready to adore the Saviour they shall soon see.*

A PASTORAL SCENE *shows the musical instruments shepherds took with them to amuse themselves and calm their flocks. The shepherds in this French woodcut of 1497 have a bagpipe and, lying on the ground (right), two flutes. The Biblical herders also played pipes and small harps.*

A SOUND
OF MUSIC
IN THE FIELDS

For most of the year the shepherd's only company was his flock. During shearing time he might meet other herders at the dipping pool and with them celebrate the harvest of fleece, but otherwise he would avoid coming on land where others had been. He sought hills and valleys that were fresh, where the grass was uncropped.

Music helped the shepherd to pass his time, and he often led his flock while playing his flute. At evening, when he had sheltered the sheep, he played and sang.

So, artists of the Middle Ages, portraying the shepherds, gave them instruments to play on. And, since the artists saw history in terms of

their own times, they painted medieval forms of ancient instruments and dressed the Biblical herdsmen in medieval peasant clothes. In one Nativity play, a flute was the shepherds' first gift to Jesus. "There! Take it in thy hand! Wherein much pleasure have I found; and now . . . Thou shalt have it to make thee mirth."

A PIPING SHEPHERD *dances to his tune while a milkmaid milks and a dog bays at angels overhead. The landscape and the herder's life are romanticized in this 15th Century miniature.*

TWO HERDERS *peer into the manger in which Jesus lies. The setting and gestures are realistic in this Dutch wood carving of about 1500.*

THE SHEPHERDS AT THE MANGER

In Bethlehem the shepherds came to the stable, and in the stable they found Joseph, Mary and the Child, and they adored the Child. Jesus lay, according to an apocryphal tale, between an ox and an ass, and the animals too worshiped Him.

The scene inspired art and legend, for in the stable, God, man and the beasts of the earth were harmoniously and simply joined in gladness.

In many countries it became popular belief that on Christmas Eve, asses and oxen could speak and that then, as Shakespeare wrote, "the bird of dawning singeth all night long . . . the nights are wholesome, then no planets strike . . . so hallowed, and so gracious is the time." For the Nativity was the birth of hope; and the shepherds, having seen Jesus, left "glorifying and praising God."

AN ANGEL GUIDE *brings a shepherd to the place of Jesus' birth. The shepherd lifts his hand in wonder while, behind him, his companions watch the cloud of angels hovering overhead. Painted in the late 1400s by Crivelli, this masterpiece combines a formal style with an air of enchantment that seems to spread across the landscape and yet center in the shining Child.*

The Ox and the Ass

The Bible mentions no animals at Jesus' birth, but writers of apocryphal books often added the beasts. This example is from "Pseudo-Matthew."

Now on the third day after the nativity of our Lord Jesus Christ, the most blessed Mary went out of the cave, and, entering a stable, put her child in a manger, and the ox and ass adored him. Then was fulfilled that which was spoken by Isaiah the prophet, who said, The ox doth know his owner, and the ass his master's crib. The very animals, therefore, ox and ass, having him between them, incessantly adored him. Then was fulfilled that which was spoken by Habakkuk the prophet, who said, Between two animals thou art made known. In the same place Joseph tarried with Mary three days.

THE FRIENDLY BEASTS

This bit of Middle Ages' doggerel takes the assumption that animals were present at the nativity one step further: Its simple quatrains endow the animals with speech and generosity.

Jesus our Brother, kind and good,
Was humbly born in a stable rude,
And the friendly beasts around Him stood;
Jesus our Brother, kind and good.

"O," said the donkey, shaggy and brown,
"I carried His mother up hill and down;
I carried His mother to Bethlehem town."
"O," said the donkey, shaggy and brown.

"O," said the cow, all white and red,
"I gave Him my manger for His bed,
I gave Him my hay to pillow His head."
"O," said the cow, all white and red.

"O," said the sheep, with curly horn,
"I gave Him my wool for His blanket warm,
He wore my coat on Christmas morn."
"O," said the sheep, with curly horn.

Thus ev'ry beast by some good spell,
In the stable dark was glad to tell
Of the gift he gave Emmanuel,
The gift he gave Emmanuel.

The Gifts

With no scriptural justification, shepherds are often depicted as presenting gifts to Christ. But what would these poor and humble men have to give? The dialogue below, which comes from a 1480 calendar, "Le Grant Kalendrier des Bergiers," imagines the rough shepherds debating which of their meager possessions to proffer.

Aloris: Shepherds, we must think of everything. I am well advised we have not yet decided what gifts, and in what fashion, we will give to this Infant, when we see Him there.

Ysambert: Aloris, that is well said. We must think of it now.

Pellion: For myself, I have well decided what present I shall give, and a worthy one.

Rifflart: What, I pray you?

Pellion: Guess, and you will hear a good answer.

Rifflart: Will you give your crook? Or your fine rosary?

Pellion: You have not guessed. My crook is too necessary, I can do nothing without it; I doubt if He will get that.

Rifflart: Will you give Him your dog?

Pellion: Nenny, who would turn my sheep home for me?

Rifflart: Then you will give Him your stale bread, and a great heap of chestnuts?

Pellion: Nenny.

Rifflart: What will you give, then?

Pellion: I will give Him my flageolet, my new one; He cannot refuse it; it was never in Betlem before except when a little packman carried it: it cost me two good deniers . . .

Ysambert: I have thought of another gift—I will give Him a rattle marvellously well made, which goes *clic, clic,* at His ear, at least when the Infant cries this rattle will dry His tears, and He will be pacified.

Aloris: I will give Him something different—I have a fine kalendar in wood which tells the days and months, Lent and the new year: by it I can tell all feasts, I have never found a truer; every saint in it has his own picture. That will be an advantage to Him; at least when He is old enough, He may learn to read it.

Rifflart: It is a gift worth having, and worthy of being given to a Count; but for my part I am determined to give Him this little bell which hangs in my hat ever since the time of Robin Fouet; and with this, a very fine whirligig which I have in my bag.

The Carol of the Bagpipers

Every year just before Christmas, shepherd "zampognari" (bagpipers) from the mountains of Italy wander through the streets of Naples playing carols at roadside shrines.

While shep-herds watch did keep, O'er all their drows-ing sheep, From heav'n a voice came sing - - ing___: "Peace, Good-will be-fall." Come and a- dore___ him, Kneel down be-fore___ Him: Seek___ the Babe___ in yon - der stall. Your King tho weak___ and small, For He this night a last - - ing___ Light now shines for all.

VI
THE STORY OF THE MAGI

NOW WHEN JESUS WAS BORN IN Bethlehem of Judaea in the days of Herod the king, behold, there came wise men from the east to Jerusalem, Saying, Where is he that is born King of the Jews? for we have seen his star in the east, and are come to worship him. …Then Herod, when he had privily called the wise men, inquired of them diligently what time the star appeared. And he sent them to Bethlehem and said, Go and search diligently for the young child; and when ye have found him, bring me word again, that I may come and worship him also. When they had heard the king, they departed; and, lo, the star, which they saw in the east, went before them, till it came and stood over where the young child was. When they saw the star, they rejoiced with exceeding great joy. And when they were come into the house, they saw the young child with Mary his mother, and fell down, and worshipped him: and when they had opened their treasures, they presented unto him gifts; gold, and frankincense, and myrrh.

MATTHEW, 2:1-2, 7-11

RICHLY ROBED *in the garb of a Floren-tine noble, a Wise Man is shown riding to the manger in this 15th Century work.*

ROYAL JOURNEY TO BETHLEHEM

THE RENDEZVOUS *of the Kings at a crossroads outside Paris is fancifully shown in the famous Duc de Berry Book of Hours.*

WHEN it became known that the Son of God was born to Mary, both rich and poor bowed in worship to Him. At one end of the scale were the shepherds mentioned in Luke, humbly adoring in the manner of simple folk everywhere. At the other end were the figures Matthew calls Wise Men (called in other sources Magi), whose reverence has come to symbolize the submission of worldly power to Christ's divine authority. The brief account in Matthew (condensed on the previous page) is the only mention of these Wise Men in the Bible. It does not name them, say where they came from or even how many there were.

Gradually, over a long period of years after Matthew's account was written, a remarkable thing occurred: the Wise Men began to take on individuality. Each acquired a name, a background, a life story. Still subsidiary in the Christmas drama, they took on leading roles in a legend of their own. They were venerated on a Church holiday—Epiphany—January 6, at first commemorated as the anniversary of the baptism of Christ but later celebrated in many lands as Three Kings Day as well. Well past the Renaissance the grip of the Magi on the popular mind kept growing, for one reason: people wanted to believe the story.

The appeal of the Magi is magical. To them alone, the Bible states, appeared the star miraculously heralding Christ's birth. Responding as to a command, they set forth with exotic gifts. The star guided them surely, while Herod the king had to ask them to bring him word of where Jesus lay. And when divine intervention kept them from revealing His location, Christ's life was saved, for Herod had professed a desire to worship the newcomer but actually meant to slay Him.

On this scriptural framework the legend was embroidered by churchmen and by lay students, authors, artists, composers. One step was to transform "wise men" into "kings." The original word "Magi" in the Latin version of the Scriptures refers to Persian priest-astrologers; later embellishments added the meaning of men of wisdom—doctors or philosophers. But in the Second Century the scholar Tertullian linked the Magi with two Old Testament prophecies that kings bearing gifts would come to Israel. By the end of the Sixth Century, "kings" and "Magi" were used interchangeably.

At about the same time the Magi became Kings, their number was being settled. Early Church art shows either two or four. St. Augustine favored 12, for its symbolic connotation of the number of the tribes of Israel and Christ's Apostles. Then papal choice in the Second Century settled on three because Matthew mentions three gifts.

By the Eighth Century the Kings had names and physical attributes. Melchior was seen as an old man, Balthazar as mature and Gaspar as a young man. Each was given a domain. Balthazar, for example, was identified with Ethiopia and frequently depicted as a Negro.

These and many other details were collected about 1370 in *The Story of the Three Kings* by a monk, John of Hildesheim. A comparable account appears in *The Golden Legend,* an earlier work by Jacobus de Voragine. Both narratives, while differing in particulars, agree on the broad outline of the legends.

In John's account the Magi met on their journey to the manger near the hill of Calvary and, despite their diverse origins, spoke freely with each other in a common tongue. Together they traveled on until they came to "the little house where Christ was. . . ." John says, "He was somewhat fat."

Contemporary paintings may well have inspired such descriptions. As the legend spread, artists undertook to visualize its meaningful moments with brush or chisel. Each came to his subject differently, and sometimes the result was more elegant than pious. Most, however, were moved by the spirit of the Magi legend: the reverent adoration of the Christ child by the three Wise Men.

THE THREE KINGS AND HEROD *are dramatically portrayed in this sculpture in the cathedral at Ulm, Germany. Herod, at right, admonished the Kings to return and tell him where they found Jesus, so that he too might go and worship Him. The Kings (crowned figures at center), unaware that Herod planned to kill Jesus, agreed to his demand. But later an angel told them of the danger.*

ORNATE CONTAINERS *for the gifts of the Magi are singled out from a Dutch painting of the 1500s. Above: round box for the gold.*

VESSEL FOR FRANKINCENSE *probably duplicates an actual metal piece, perhaps a ceremonial container for church or court use.*

URN FOR MYRRH *is in Balthazar's hand. Melchior usually is first in line, giving the gold, Gaspar to one side with frankincense.*

THE REGAL GIFTS OF THE MAGI

The presentation of their gifts to Jesus and their adoration of Him—at once the aim and the climax of the Kings' journey—have moved men's minds for centuries. Kneeling in tribute *(opposite),* the Magi express the love and awe Christ evokes in all who believe in Him.

What gifts were judged suitable to such a moment? The Bible names them: gold, frankincense and myrrh. Each has its obvious worth. Gold is a valuable metal; frankincense and myrrh are aromatic resins from the bark of African trees *(right),* valued for incense. Beyond these practical purposes are rich symbolic meanings.

Many church scholars consider the gold to mean love or Christ as King of the world; the frankincense (a very sweet spice), prayer or Christ as King of Heaven; the myrrh (from a thorny tree), suffering or a symbol of Christ's approaching sacrifice. Jacobus de Voragine suggests pragmatically that the gold was intended to ease Mary's poverty, the frankincense to ward off stable smells and the myrrh to deter the stable's vermin.

FRANKINCENSE   MYRRH

Since the Bible does not mention containers for the gifts, artists created them. A small casket often is shown for gold coins, a vessel for frankincense, an urn for myrrh.

At some point in the development of the Magi legend, its central figures passed into folklore and were made responsible for distributing gifts to good children on Three Kings Day. In most lands this Christmas function ultimately fell to Santa Claus, St. Nicholas or some other personage, but the Kings still delight children in most of Spain and Spanish America. Their first gifts to Jesus—love and devotion—set a pattern now almost universal on Christ's birthday.

KNEELING KINGS *appear in a detail of a mosaic by Pietro Cavallini (about 1290) in Rome's Santa Maria Church in Trastevere.*

"ADORATION OF THE MAGI" was done in oil by Sandro Botticelli about 1480 (next pages). Before a classical structure in an Italian landscape surrounded by shepherds and attendants in contemporary Florentine dress, the Three Kings offer their traditional gifts to the infant Jesus. Though the artist was tempted to produce a scene of fashionable pageantry, a quietly reverent mood prevails. Besides paintings by Renaissance masters, the Adoration of the Magi has been rendered in graphic media from stained glass to whalebone by artists all over the world.

AFTER BETHLEHEM

According to Matthew, the Wise Men were "warned in a dream" not to go back to Herod after seeing Jesus in Bethlehem, so "they departed into their own country another way." The stylized 12th Century stone carving above, credited to Gislebertus and found in the Cathedral of St.-Lazare in Autun, France, shows the Kings, three in a bed and serene of mind as an angel awakens them with God's warning. This sleep scene later came

to be considered undignified and was not depicted after the 16th Century.

The Bible is silent on the Kings after their departure for home. Not so John of Hildesheim, whose imaginative account (excerpted on the following pages) includes their death and burial in one tomb. Historically, three bodies said to be the Kings were taken from Milan to Cologne in 1164. A handsome shrine was erected and the "Three Kings of Cologne" attracted visitors from all Europe. Both the shrine and the bodies now are vanished, and with them much belief in this legend of the Magi. Still the tradition lives on and continues to enrich the Christmas story.

What Befell the Kings Later

John of Hildesheim, already cited in this chapter, made the definitive collection of the legends that had been accumulating for centuries about the Three Kings. This work was done at some point between 1364, when the Bishop of Münster asked the Carmelite monk to undertake it, and 1373, the year John died. "The Story of the Three Kings" was written in Latin, later translated into other languages. The English version from which the excerpt below was taken is an adaptation by Margaret Freeman. It takes the Kings from India (where astrologers allegedly had watched from the Hill of Vaus for a star that would herald the Messiah) along their several roads to Jerusalem. It has them meeting the shepherds and presenting gifts to them before going on to the stable where Jesus lay and offering Him gold, frankincense and myrrh. Then the book follows them home again and, in the chapters below, tells how they founded a city called Suwella, chose Prester John to rule there, then died—all probably imaginary, but described with faith and love. The illustrations used here are from woodcuts in an edition of "The Three Kings" printed in Strasbourg in 1484.

Then these three Kings with all their people went with Saint Thomas the Apostle to the Hill of Vaus; and there Saint Thomas hallowed the chapel that the three Kings had built there. And Saint Thomas and these three Kings preached to the people in that chapel concerning the Christian faith and the star that had appeared to the three Kings.

And the fame of these three Kings and of Saint Thomas spread to all the lands about and so great was their renown that all manner of men and women came from divers countries to visit the chapel on the Hill of Vaus. And from the great concourse of people that came to this chapel, the three Kings ordained a fair city and a rich one, which is called Suwella.

God is evermore wonderful in his work, for when Saint Thomas had thus preached and converted the people to the Christian belief, then he ordained and consecrated these three Kings as archbishops. And they then ordained other bishops, priests and clerks to serve God. Also Saint Thomas taught them all the manner and form of saying mass; also he taught them the words that Christ had said at supper the night that he was betrayed, and the Paternoster and many other things. He told them also the form of baptising and especially he charged them that they should never forget that. And when Saint Thomas had informed these three Kings and all the other people of the faith, then he went forth to other cities and towns and preached. And then he suffered martyrdom for the love of Christ.

And ye shall understand that in that country where Saint Thomas was slain, both men and women have visages like hounds.

After the death of Saint Thomas these three Kings who were archbishops did hallow all the temples in the country to the worship of Our Lady and cast out all the idols in the temples and ordained bishops and priests and clerks. And to these bishops, priests and clerks the three

Kings gave many possessions to maintain God's service.

Then these three Kings forsook the vanity of the world and abode in the city of Suwella, which they had founded, as it was aforesaid, and all the people about them did venerate them and love them.

And the second year before the death of these

three Kings they did call together all the kings and princes and bishops of their lands, for they were now in the last age of their lives and they had no children nor heirs; neither had they ever had queens or concubines as is the common usage of all the country. And this is found in all the writings and books of the East, though a German chronicler says the contrary of Melchior, who, according to these writings, had a wife and by her a child.

And when all the people were gathered together, the three Kings, with the assent of the people, chose a man among them who should be spiritual head in Saint Thomas' place and who should be called Patriarch Thomas. And the first patriarch that was thus chosen was a man called Jacob who had come with Saint Thomas from Antioch to India.

When the Patriarch Thomas was thus chosen, then these three Kings with the common assent of all the people chose and ordained a worshipful and mighty lord who should be temporal head and governor. And they ordained that this lord should not be called King or Emperor but Prester John, in veneration of Saint John the Evangelist and also Saint John the Baptist. And so the names of these lords continue yet unto this day.

And when this was done all the people went home again with great joy and these three Kings abode still in the city of Suwella.

N ow these three Kings lived together for two more years in the city of Suwella which they had founded near the Hill of Vaus. Then a little while before the feast of the Nativity of Our Lord Jesus Christ there appeared a wonderful star above the city, by which star the three Kings understood that the time was nigh when they should pass out of this world. Wherefore they did make a fair great tomb for their burial in the same church that they had there ordained. And in that same church these three Kings on the feast of Christmas did celebrate solemnly divine service.

Now on the eighth day after the birth of Christ, Melchior, who was King of Arabia and Nubia, said mass solemnly in the church, and at that time he was a hundred and sixteen years old. And when he had said mass he laid himself down, and without any disease, he yielded up to Our Lord God his spirit and so died. And the other two Kings came and took his body and arrayed it with bishops' ornaments and bore him to his tomb and there they laid him.

Then on the feast of the Epiphany, Balthasar, who was King of Saba, said devoutly his mass. And when mass was done, without any grievance he

passed out of this world to the bliss that is everlasting. And the years of his age were a hundred and twelve. So Jaspar, the third King, and other men took up this King, and when they had arrayed him as he should be, they laid him beside Melchior, his fellow, in the same tomb.

And then the sixth day after that, Jaspar, who was King of Tharsis, when he had offered the blessed sacrament on the altar and with all devotion had said his mass, then Christ took to him his spirit to dwell with him in everlasting joy. And so before all the people he died. And the years of his age were a

hundred and nine. Then the people came and took his body and arrayed it worshipfully and bore it to the same tomb where these other two Kings lay. And then this wonder Christ showed there before all the people: when the body of the third King was brought to be laid in the tomb beside the two Kings, anon each one of the two Kings moved apart from the other and gave room for Jaspar in the middle place.

And so as these three glorious Kings lived together in life, they were not parted in their death. And these three Kings in their tomb seemed to the people not as dead bodies but as men who were asleep. And they remained whole and incorrupt many years and days afterwards.

And the star that appeared over the city before their death abode there always still, until the bodies of the three Kings were moved away.

A long time after the death of these three Kings the Christian faith stood and was in prosperity in the worshipful city of Suwella and in all the Kingdoms of the East. Then the devil through his wicked angels excited among the people divers errors and opinions of heresy in the lands of the East, and also in Suwella where these three Kings rested. And the people turned again to their old law and worshipped false gods and forsook the law of God; so that these three Kings were held in no reverence and were almost forgotten. And whereas their bodies had remained incorrupt before, now they dissolved and turned into powder.

And those people dwelling at that time in Suwella who had come from the lands and kingdoms of these three Kings, each group took its King out of the tomb and put him into a separate chest and bore him home to his own land and kingdom. And there each King remained for a long time afterward, each in his own country.

JOURNEY OF THE MAGI

From the quaintness of John of Hildesheim to the realism of T.S. Eliot seems a far cry, but the modern poet shared John's interest in myth. In the work below he adds a disturbing philosophical consideration to the story of the Magi.

"A cold coming we had of it,
Just the worst time of the year
For a journey, and such a long journey:
The ways deep and the weather sharp,
The very dead of winter."
And the camels galled, sore-footed, refractory,
Lying down in the melting snow.
There were times we regretted
The summer palaces on slopes, the terraces,
And the silken girls bringing sherbet.
Then the camel men cursing and grumbling
And running away, and wanting their liquor and women,
And the night-fires going out, and the lack of shelters,
And the cities hostile and the towns unfriendly
And the villages dirty and charging high prices:
A hard time we had of it.
At the end we preferred to travel all night,
Sleeping in snatches,
With the voices singing in our ears, saying
That this was all folly.

Then at dawn we came down to a temperate valley,
Wet, below the snow line, smelling of vegetation;
With a running stream and a water-mill beating the darkness,
And three trees on the low sky,
And an old white horse galloped away in the meadow.
Then we came to a tavern with vine-leaves over the lintel,
Six hands at an open door dicing for pieces of silver,
And feet kicking the empty wine-skins.
But there was no information, and so we continued
And arrived at evening, not a moment too soon
Finding the place; it was (you may say) satisfactory.

All this was a long time ago, I remember,
And I would do it again, but set down
This set down
This: were we led all that way for
Birth or Death? There was a Birth, certainly,
We had evidence and no doubt. I had seen birth and death,
But had thought they were different; this Birth was
Hard and bitter agony for us, like Death, our death.
We returned to our places, these Kingdoms,
But no longer at ease here, in the old dispensation,
With an alien people clutching their gods.
I should be glad of another death.

This 19th Century work by Henry Wadsworth Longfellow is traditional in form and thought in its treatment of the theme of the Kings. The passage below is taken from a poem whose special appeal lies in its sensuous imagery.

Three Kings came riding from far away,
Melchior and Gaspar and Baltasar;
Three Wise Men out of the East were they,
And they travelled by night and they slept by day,
For their guide was a beautiful, wonderful star...
Three caskets they bore on their saddle-bows,
Three caskets of gold with golden keys;
Their robes were of crimson silk, with rows
Of bells and pomegranates and furbelows,
Their turbans like blossoming almond-trees...
They laid their offerings at his feet:
The gold was their tribute to a King;
The frankincense, with its odor sweet,
Was for the Priest, the Paraclete;
The myrrh for the body's burying.

Nicolas Roi Mage

The magic of the Three Kings' story has captured the imagination of all ages. This account of a fourth Wise Man is the work of the French author Roger Vercel (1894-1957), translated and adapted by Audrey Foote.

We were celebrating Epiphany at the home of my friend, Dr. Herve, and I had found the bean in my portion of the cake. I extricated the bean from the cake and held it up, careful to assume that particular expression, both smug and idiotic, which is considered proper form on such an occasion. The usual ritual followed: the choice of a queen and then toasts, punctuated with the traditional "The King Drinks!" The doctor had watched this playful ceremony with noticeable distraction. Suddenly he remarked,

"This reminds me that I once knew a Mage."

"Ah! Which of the three?" I asked.

"The fourth," Herve answered.

And then he told us the following story:

It was 12 years ago, and I had just arrived in Brittany. Like so many young men starting out, I had a little second-hand automobile. It was a sturdy enough little car but one fine night in December it stopped dead, right in the middle of the barren countryside.

A half hour passed during which I loosened a screw here, cleaned off a wire there; alternating with this routine, I tried spinning the crank. Nothing worked. Already night was falling and I began to wonder nervously if another turn of the crank might get it started or whether I would have to go through it all again in the pitch dark; I straightened up once more from under the hood to find standing beside me a bizarre figure, watching me.

He was a man of about 50 with a grey beard and long hair. He was thin as a lath. He was dressed in a shirt and trousers like those of a harlequin, made of various scraps of material but sewn together with care.

I admit that this encounter, in that solitude, was disquieting. The immobility, the silence of the man —appearing out of nowhere—were not reassuring. I did what one does in such cases: I pretended not to notice this strange spectator and I began again to crank the engine with redoubled energy and no success.

The bizarre figure beside me suddenly said, "There's something wrong with the ignition."

I had begun to suspect as much, but it greatly pleased me to hear *him* say it. Somehow the remark stripped him of mystery and clothed him in an air of reassuring normality.

He added, "I've played around some with motors; would you like me to look at it?"

He was welcome to try, I said. As I had done, he loosened a screw, cleaned a wire, but apparently in the right places. "Now it has some juice."

And, in fact, the engine started at the first try. I thanked my good samaritan with true gratitude. But his next remark jolted me back to my first feelings of disquiet:

"It's a good thing this didn't happen a half hour later for I wouldn't have been here to fix it; it's the hour when I enter the Throne Room."

This declaration rendered the countryside, already darkening, more hostile and menacing than ever. I repeated a hasty thanks, bounded into the seat and drove off with a sensation of deliverance.

Naturally I spoke to my acquaintances of my encounter.

"Ah," they said. "You have met Nicolas."

I learned that my mechanic was a former sailor who had literally fallen on his head; one day on a voyage to Newfoundland he had toppled head first from the mainmast where he was reefing a tops'l. Since then, he became a King every night as soon as he fell asleep.

Understand me: he was not crazy. But whereas *our* dreams are varied and unrelated, he took up the same dream each night and at the very point he had left it the night before. And in his dream, this simple peasant led the existence of an oriental King.

"He doesn't like summer," my friends said. "The nights are too short."

Thus acquainted with his case, I made certain I saw him often.

I do not believe that there could exist a happier being than that one, for whom daily life was but a negligible incident, and who saw open each night the doors of a magical domain. I even began to envy him a little, comparing his nights with my own; for I was often awakened by the frantic ring of the doorbell and would have to set out, only half awake, to grope my way through the dirty little streets of the village.

Despite his regal, second life, Nicolas was troubled. One night in January I found him agitated to the point of frenzy. Things were not going well at the Palace. Certain envious persons were trying to overthrow him, to suborn his servants and his guards, to put themselves on his throne. But if they were looking for a fight, they'd find one! There would be a real brawl, even if it meant the end of him.

This fantasy revolution struck me as a very real menace; I realized immediately that Nicolas risked violent madness. I sought, without finding, the means to rescue him.

I had to leave him on the doorstep of his cottage, somber, tense, ready for sleep, but this time to confront the terrifying enemies which his dream would call forth. I went straight to the parsonage and I recounted the whole affair to the curé.

"If you have an idea, abbé—"

He *had* an idea, and it was a good one.

He went to find Nicolas and said to him:

"If I were in your place, do you know what I would do? I would depart immediately for Bethlehem. It will soon be Epiphany; this is the moment when the Kings begin their journey. I would gather around me all the loyal fellows I could find —there must be a few left?"

"Yes," Nicolas admitted. "I still have a few loyal buddies."

"Well then!" said the abbé. "I would lead them right off to Bethlehem. One couldn't lose one's way; one has only to follow the star. And once there, I'm sure I would be well received. And to come and bother me there with the baby Jesus? Just let them try! . . . There were only three kings so you will be the fourth and that will be all to the good: I have always thought that Brittany ought to have sent someone."

Nicolas left that very night for the crèche with his entourage. And as the abbé had predicted, he was well received, so well in fact that when I saw him again I found him radiant, his face all illuminated from within.

Once arrived at the crèche, he stayed there—for he died on Chandeleur. I never saw a sweeter death. His last words were:

"The Little One will be content."

And, without being in on the secrets of heaven, I believe the "Little One" was content.

Frankincense and Myrrh

Many writers have taken liberties in interpreting the gifts and the personalities of the three Wise Men. In the following story, the American newspaperman Heywood Broun (1888-1939) invents another present for Jesus—a gift that proves one of the Wise Men truly wise.

Once there were three kings in the East and they were wise men. They read the heavens and they saw a certain strange star by which they knew that in a distant land the King of the World was to be born. The star beckoned to them and they made preparations for a long journey.

From their palaces they gathered rich gifts, gold and frankincense and myrrh. Great sacks of precious stuffs were loaded on the backs of the camels which were to bear them on their journey. Everything was in readiness, but one of the wise men seemed perplexed and would not come at once to join his two companions, who were eager and impatient to be on their way in the direction indicated by the star.

They were old, these two kings, and the other wise man was young. When they asked him he could not tell why he waited. He knew that his treasures had been ransacked for rich gifts for the King of Kings. It seemed that there was nothing more which he could give, and yet he was not content.

He made no answer to the old men who shouted to him that the time had come. The camels were impatient and swayed and snarled. The shadows across the desert grew longer. And still the young king sat and thought deeply.

At length he smiled, and he ordered his servants to open the great treasure sack upon the back of the first of his camels. Then he went into a high chamber to which he had not been since he was a child. He rummaged about and presently came out and approached the caravan. In his hand he carried something which glinted in the sun.

The kings thought that he carried some new gift more rare and precious than any which they had been able to find in all their treasure rooms. They bent down to see, and even the camel drivers peered from the backs of the great beasts to find out what it was which gleamed in the sun. They were curious about this last gift for which all the caravan had waited.

And the young king took a toy from his hand and placed it upon the sand. It was a dog of tin, painted white, and speckled with black spots. Great patches of paint had worn away and left the metal clear, and that was why the toy shone in the sun as if it had been silver.

The youngest of the wise men turned a key in the side of the little black and white dog and then he stepped aside so that the kings and the camel drivers could see. The dog leaped high in the air and turned a somersault. He turned another and another and then fell over on his side and lay there with a set and painted grin upon his face.

A child, the son of a camel driver, laughed and clapped his hands, but the kings were stern. They rebuked the youngest of the wise men and he paid no attention but called to his chief servant to make the first of all the camels kneel. Then he picked up the toy of tin and, opening the treasure sack, placed his last gift with his own hands in the mouth of the sack so that it rested safely upon the soft bags of incense.

"What folly has seized you?" cried the eldest of the wise men. "Is this a gift to bear to the King of Kings in the far country?"

And the young man answered and said: "For the King of Kings there are gifts of great richness, gold and frankincense and myrrh.

"But this," he said, "is for the child in Bethlehem."

The Golden Carol of the Three Wise Men

One of the oldest English carols, hard to date but suggesting medieval music in its persistent rhythmic motion, is the "Golden Carol" sung on Twelfth Night. Many such carols originated as the music announcing the Three Kings in various medieval miracle and mystery plays.

We saw a light shine out a-far, On Christmas in the morn-ing.
And straight we knew it was Christ's star, Bright beam-ing in the morn-ing.

Then did we fall on bend-ed knee, On Christmas in the morn-ing,

And praised the Lord, who'd let us see His glo-ry at its dawn-ing.

VII

A LEGACY OF LOVE

IN THE BEGINNING WAS THE Word, and the Word was with God, and the Word was God. The same was in the beginning with God. All things were made by him; and without him was not any thing made that was made. In him was life; and the life was the light of men. And the light shineth in darkness; and the darkness comprehended it not. . . . He came unto his own, and his own received him not. But as many as received him, to them gave he power to become the sons of God, even to them that believe on his name: Which were born, not of blood, nor of the will of the flesh, nor of the will of man, but of God. And the Word was made flesh, and dwelt among us, (and we beheld his glory, the glory as of the only begotten of the Father,) full of grace and truth. JOHN, 1:1-5, 11-14

CHRIST'S ASCENSION *fulfills the promise of His birth. Seen opposite is Giotto's version, a 1305 fresco in the Arena Chapel at Padua.*

A LIFE,
A LESSON
FOR MANKIND

JESUS IN TRIUMPH *enters Jerusalem, as prophesied by Zechariah. The Latin echoes Zechariah, "In the eighth month. . . ."*

CHRISTMASTIDE ends with Epiphany. This is the manifestation of Christ to the Gentiles, in the persons of the Magi. Thus the close of Christmas opens the greater narrative of Christ's life, His ministry and His legacy to all mankind.

The Gospels tell us little about Jesus' early years. The Holy Family fled from Bethlehem into Egypt to escape the efforts of King Herod to destroy "the young child" who the wise men had told him was "born King of the Jews." After the death of Herod (when Jesus was two or three), the Holy Family went back to Joseph's hometown of Nazareth. There "the child grew, and waxed strong in spirit, filled with wisdom; and the grace of God was upon him."

Joseph was a carpenter. Medieval tradition had it that he died when Jesus was 19, and that the young man took over the business. Some scholars think He may have been influenced by the Essenes, the sect which composed and preserved the manuscripts now known as the Dead Sea Scrolls. No one knows. What *is* known is that

His time was an age of change. Both the Judaic and Roman cultures had fallen under the influence of Hellenism, and the Roman system was showing the first signs of the interior corruption that would later cause its military defeat. It was an apocalyptic time, ripe for the coming of the Messiah who would restore Israel as a great nation.

In those days came John the Baptist, preaching in the wilderness of Judea, And saying, Repent ye: for the kingdom of heaven is at hand." John, the son of Mary's cousin Elizabeth, was, in fulfillment of Isaiah's prophecy, the "voice of him that crieth in the wilderness, Prepare ye the way of the Lord." He baptized Jesus, and "lo, the heavens were opened unto him, and he saw the Spirit of God descending like a dove, and lighting upon him: And lo a voice from heaven, saying, This is my beloved Son, in whom I am well pleased."

Christ's ministry had begun. But He brought not the promise of a political kingdom for one nation, but the gospel of the kingdom of God, which is "within you."

Jesus' ministry took the form of deeds and words. The deeds, demonstrations of His boundless love, mercy and charity, are often miracles of healing—of the blind and dumb, of the palsied and lame, of lepers and madmen, and of the dead restored to life. They are demonstrations of the power of love and hope combined. "Thy faith hath made thee whole," said Christ.

The words of Christ's ministry are outwardly simple, concerned with homely subjects—bread and wine, fishing and farming—but they carry a revolutionary message. Jesus stated: "Verily, verily, I say unto thee, Except a man be born again, he

cannot see the kingdom of God."

His teaching was grounded solidly in the Old Testament. "Thou shalt love the Lord thy God with all thy heart, and with all thy soul, and with all thy mind. This is the first and great commandment. And the second is like unto it, Thou shalt love thy neighbor as thyself. On these two commandments hang all the law and the prophets."

"Think not that I am come to destroy the law, or the prophets," He declared in the Sermon on the Mount, "I am not come to destroy, but to fulfill." In fulfilling, he refined and transformed the old precepts: "It hath been said, Thou shalt love thy neighbor, and hate thine enemy. But I say unto you, Love your enemies, bless them that curse you, do good to them that hate you, and pray for them which despitefully use you, and persecute you."

This is a demanding doctrine but one which excludes no one: "I say unto you that . . . joy shall be in heaven over one sinner that repenteth, more than over ninety and nine just persons, which need no repentance."

For those who would not obey the commands of His teaching, Christ foresaw "outer darkness . . . weeping and gnashing of teeth." But to the humble, the merciful—to all erring human beings who truly repent —He made the promise: "Ask, and it shall be given you; seek, and ye shall find; knock, and it shall be opened unto you."

Christ's words (John 15:11) sum up the essence of Christianity. "These things have I spoken unto you, that my joy might remain in you, and that your joy might be full. This is my commandment, That ye love one another as I have loved you."

That is Christ's legacy to mankind.

"THE HEAD OF CHRIST," *by Georges Rouault, shows a compassionate Jesus who might be saying, "Suffer the little children to come unto me and forbid them not: for of such is the Kingdom of God." One of a large number of heads of Jesus painted by Rouault in the late 1930s, this one is owned by the Cleveland Museum of Art. Many in the same series show Christ being mocked.*

MIRACLES
AND MYSTERIES

At the heart of Christianity is faith in the miracle of God's incarnation in the Son of Man and of the Son of Man's triumph over death. The theme has inspired countless paintings, many as radiantly mystical as these three panels from the great altarpiece painted about 1515 by the German master Grünewald. The altarpiece is now displayed in the Unterlinden Museen in Colmar, France.

In the panel at the left, Grünewald portrays the Annunciation. As the angel Gabriel appears, and the dove

of the Holy Spirit hovers in the background of the little chapel, Mary's Bible opens to the prophecy of Isaiah: "Behold, a virgin shall conceive, and bear a son. . . ." Above her, a sculptured figure of Isaiah waits for the fulfillment of his prophecy.

The central panel depicts two Nativity scenes. Within the shrine (rear), Mary, surrounded by angelic musicians, awaits the birth of the Child. In the foreground, she holds the newborn Christ, while the celestial host proclaims the tidings of great joy.

In the panel at the right, the Resurrection marks the ultimate triumph of the spirit. Christ, enveloped in a divine radiance, rises from the tomb into the starry firmament, a token to all who will receive Him of hope and deliverance for all of mankind.

CHRIST'S LIFE, A GIFT TO THE WORLD

Throughout the Middle Ages the art that adorned every church helped to familiarize the people with the details of the Gospel stories as well as to keep a constant reminder before the faithful. This remarkable example is a pictorial biography of Christ —not unlike a comic strip in form. Now in the Berlin-Dahlem Staatliche Museen, it was painted about 1400 by a German artist known only as the Cologne Master. Thirty-four of the panels pertain to Christ, the 35th shows the work's donors. From left to right, the scenes are:

Top row: 1) The Annunciation; 2) The Visitation; 3) Mary and Joseph Going to Bethlehem; 4) The Manger; 5) The Circumcision; 6) The Adoration of the Magi; 7) The Presentation in the Temple.

Second row: 1) Christ in the Temple at 12; 2) His Childhood *(top)* and Baptism *(bottom);* 3) Christ Preaching; 4) The Entry into Jerusalem; 5) The Last Supper; 6) Christ Washing the Disciples' Feet; 7) The Agony in the Garden.

Third row: 1) The Awakening of the Apostles; 2) The Kiss of Judas; 3) Christ before Herod; 4) Christ before the High Priest; 5) Christ before Pilate; 6) The Scourging; 7) The Crown of Thorns.

Fourth row: 1) Pilate Washes His Hands; 2) Christ Carrying the Cross; 3) Christ Is Disrobed; 4) Christ Is Nailed to the Cross; 5) The Crucifixion; 6) The Descent from the Cross; 7) The *Pietà,* or Mourning of the Virgin over Christ's Body.

Fifth row: 1) The Lamentation; 2) The Resurrection *(bottom)* and The Descent into Hell; 3) The Ascension of Christ; 4) The Descent of the Holy Ghost; 5) The Death of the Virgin Mary; 6) The Last Judgment; 7) Portraits of the donors, the family that originally commissioned the work.

A STORY
FOR ALL TIME

The lesson of Christ's life, like the parables, is timeless. One measure of this quality is the way in which artists of each succeeding age have retold the story in terms of their own time. Hans Memling, in *The Seven*

Joys of Mary (above), dating from about 1465 and now in the Pinako-thek at Munich, suffused the narrative with the tranquillity of the late medieval Rhineland, yet caught the vibrancy of color surging north from

Renaissance Italy. Time runs like a placid river through the painting, uniting the whole, so that each viewing reveals fresh details and new scenes. A few are *(left)* the Annunciation, the angel with the shepherds, the Nativity, and *(right)* the Resurrection and the Ascension of Christ. The Adoration of the Magi fills the center foreground, but the Wise Men are also shown approaching *(at left background)*, confronting Herod in his courtyard *(middle background)*, departing from the manger through a rocky defile and finally setting sail (as John of Hildesheim has embroidered their story) in three ships on their journey home *(background)*.

95

JOSEPHUS' TESTIMONY

Early nonscriptural works helped to spread the story of Jesus. One of the earliest and most influential of these was written by Flavius Josephus, a Jewish soldier-historian who was born in Jerusalem shortly after Christ died on Calvary. This excerpt from "Antiquities of the Jews" may have been added by another writer.

Now about this time lived Jesus, a wise man, if indeed he should be called a man. He was a doer of wonderful works, a teacher of men who receive the truth with pleasure, and won over many Jews and many Greeks. He was the Christ. And when Pilate, at the information of the leading men among us, sentenced him to the cross, those who loved him at the start did not cease to do so, for he appeared to them alive again on the third day as had been foretold—both this and ten thousand other wonderful things concerning him—by the divine prophets. Nor is the tribe of Christians, so named after him, extinct to this day.

The Letter of Lentulus

What did Jesus look like? No record exists, but writers and artists have tried hard to portray Him. Although now proved to be a 14th or 15th Century work, the description below from the so-called "Letter of Lentulus" is a plausible and enduring word picture of Christ.

Lentulus, president of the people of Jerusalem, to the Roman Senate and People: Greeting.

There has appeared in our times, and still is, a man of great virtue named Christ Jesus, who is called by the Gentiles a prophet of truth, whom his disciples call the Son of God, raising the dead and healing diseases. He is a man of lofty stature, handsome, having a venerable countenance which the beholders can both love and fear. He has wavy hair, rather crisp, of a bluish tinge, and glossy, flowing down from his shoulders, with a parting in the middle of the head after the manner of the Nazarenes. His forehead is even and very serene, and his face without any wrinkle or spot, and beautiful with a slight blush. His nose and mouth are without fault; he has a beard abundant and reddish, of the colour of his hair, not long but forked. His eyes are sparkling and bright. He is terrible in rebuke, calm and loving in admonition, cheerful but preserving gravity, has never been seen to laugh but often to weep. Thus, in stature of body, he is tall; and his hands and limbs are beautiful to look upon. In speech he is grave, reserved, and modest; and he is fair among the children of men. Farewell.

THE KINGDOM WITHIN

Of the countless writings about Christ in the past 2,000 years, few have summed up His legacy as tellingly as the passage below. It was written by the Dutch theologian Johannes Jacobus van der Leeuw (1893-1934) in "The Dramatic History of the Christian Faith."

He came without privileges of outer power or possession to further the work that He was to undertake. He had renounced all those weapons which the man of the world thinks indispensable in his struggle to achieve. He did not stoop to defend Himself when attacked; never in those short but marvellous years of His ministry did He use His superhuman powers to assert Himself. His strength throughout lay in the Kingdom within, not the kingdom without. . . .

His teaching was all woven around the Kingdom of God within, the Kingdom open to all who care to enter—and who prove their ability to fulfil the conditions of entrance. Here no privileges of money or position can bribe the guardians of the sacred Portal, here the Soul of man, alone, naked in the renunciation of all that belongs to the world without, must seek entrance in the strength not of what he has, but of what he is. Rags cannot hide, nor kingly robes impersonate that nobility of the Soul itself, which alone will admit it to the Company of the Elect, the Communion of Saints, who by virtue of their spiritual aristocracy are inhabitants of the Kingdom of God. . . .

Christ, in the crystalline perfection of a life that knew no compromise, showed the way to the Kingdom and the fruits of attainment. It is as if He set out to make clear from the beginning what is essential and what non-essential. Privileges of birth, station, wealth or power He relinquished; efforts to dominate or to convince those around Him He never made; He allowed Himself to be taken, insulted, humiliated, killed to show that all this could not bar the way to Victory. Never again could any, failing to achieve, blame misfortune or surroundings. Christ in His life took these weak excuses from us, by undergoing all we can undergo and worse, by renouncing from the outset all the weapons we might think indispensable in our quest, and conquering in the strength of the Spirit alone. . . .

That, the teaching He lived, was the essential, the new thing He gave to this world; from that spread Christianity; by that living Fire it is maintained.

Then as now the Christian Faith is centred in the living Christ, then as now His life of love and purity is the way to the Kingdom of God—the way He went, the way we follow.

Joy to the World

The 18th Century English poet Isaac Watts wrote the words (imitating the Psalms) and the 19th Century American composer Lowell Mason wrote the music (in the style of G. F. Handel) of this beloved Christmas hymn.

Joy to the World! The Lord is come: Let earth re - ceive her King; Let ev - ry heart prepare Him room, And heav'n and nature sing, And heav'n and na - ture sing, And heav'n, and heav'n, and na - ture sing.

VIII

THE WORLD REBORN

AND I SAW A NEW HEAVEN AND a new earth: for the first heaven and the first earth were passed away; and there was no more sea. And I John saw the holy city, new Jerusalem, coming down from God out of heaven, prepared as a bride adorned for her husband. And I heard a great voice out of heaven saying, Behold, the tabernacle of God is with men, and he will dwell with them, and they shall be his people, and God himself shall be with them, and be their God. And God shall wipe away all tears from their eyes; and there shall be no more death, neither sorrow, nor crying, neither shall there be any more pain: for the former things are passed away. And he that sat upon the throne said, Behold, I make all things new. And he said unto me, Write: for these words are true and faithful. And he said unto me, It is done. I am Alpha and Omega, the beginning and the end.... REVELATION, 21:1-6

A FRESH AND RENEWING FORCE

"HOW SILENTLY, how silently the wondrous gift is given." These familiar words, from the carol "O Little Town of Bethlehem," reflect some of the awe that the birth of Jesus inspires. The words suggest, also, a theological point of view. For, while Christmas is a season of great joy, theologians are quick to point out that it does not exhaust the glory of Christianity. To theologians the Nativity is a beginning whose magnitude must be judged by something that is yet to come.

What happened when Jesus was born, in the eyes of Christians, is that God became incarnate—that He assumed human flesh. "The Word was made flesh," the Gospel according to St. John says, "and dwelt among us." The full significance of the Incarnation, however, was not immediately apparent.

It was not until after the Resurrection, Christians believe, that the meaning of Christmas was unfolded.

A Catholic theologian, Monsignor Myles Bourke, explains it in this way: "We see the full significance of the Incarnation through the Resurrection. When Christ appeared His divinity was concealed behind His human nature. In the Resurrection, there is a transformation of the whole human nature of Jesus." Much the same is stated by a Protestant scholar, Professor W. D. Davies: "The birth of Jesus is the beginning of that mode of His existence which is limited spatially and chronologically. The Resurrection is the beginning of that mode of His existence in which He transcends the limitations of space and time."

The Resurrection, Christians believe, lent a new dimension to the Incarnation; God manifested Himself in human form, and by His suffering and death took man's sins upon Himself and through His Resurrection offered eternal life to those who would but believe in Him.

Incarnation and Resurrection are inextricable. As Professor Davies says: "The stories of the Nativity and the Resurrection embody the idea of the re-creation of the world."

For those who accept this idea, the world is seen afresh. The abbreviated testimony of one believer, the poet Marguerite Wilkinson, accompanies some pictures (on these and the following pages) which show the new, heightened insight into the world about us. Some of the photographs are flooded with sunlight, others clouded in mist. Some evoke a feeling of joy, others a mood of sorrow. Pictorially, they

reflect the message of Christianity.

For Christians preach a religion of joy, but behind the joy lies an awareness of sorrow. The life of Jesus drawn from the Scriptures is a story of love and salvation achieved through pain and humiliation. Thus, while the triumphant "Hallelujah Chorus" is the best-known part of Handel's oratorio *Messiah*, it is still only a part. Handel turned to the Old Testament prophet Isaiah to find words to describe what God in human flesh faced on earth. The prophet says (53:3,5), in this passage which many Christians relate to Jesus: "He is despised and rejected of men; a man of sorrows, and acquainted with grief . . . he was wounded for our transgressions, he was bruised for our iniquities."

But for Christians the sorrow is dispelled and the joy of Christmas triumphs in the final accounting. Jesus said (John 16:20): ". . . ye shall weep and lament, but the world shall rejoice: and ye shall be sorrowful, but your sorrow shall be turned into joy." For Christians believe that something new entered the world when the Child was born. And they believe that something new—a gospel of love and eternal life—is the heritage of all who will accept the love of God through Jesus. And they believe, as St. Paul wrote (Romans 8:38-39): "Neither death, nor life, nor angels, nor principalities, nor powers, nor things present, nor things to come, nor height, nor depth, nor any other creature, shall be able to separate us from the love of God, which is in Christ Jesus our Lord."

Out of the troubled dark I came...

Time narrowed then
Into an instant....
And quietly my spirit was renewed...

Time widened out into eternity;
Power was upon me so that I could see
Light beyond light...
Torrents of tumbled glory....

White rays impetuous, violet pools serene...
And a broad azure tide whose waves are curled
Around the margins of the farthest world.
Light followed darkness...

THE
GLORY
AND
PAGEANTRY
OF
CHRISTMAS

PART TWO

INTRODUCTION

A distinguished American scholar, Dr. Earl Count, has defined Christmas in these words: it is "a spontaneous drama of the common folk, a prayer, a hymn. All the while that Raphael was painting the Sistine Madonna, Frenchmen building the cathedral of Chartres, English bishops composing the Book of Common Prayer, Handel his *Messiah*, Bach his *B-Minor Mass*, the common people, out of whom these geniuses sprang, were composing Christmas."

They composed it slowly, taking years—even centuries—to complete the task. St. Nicholas, for example, was a bishop in Asia Minor in the Fourth Century. In the Middle Ages, a towering folk legend evolved which credited him with saving sailors in distress (*opposite*) and providing dowries for marriageable maidens. It was not until the 17th Century, when the Dutch who settled New Amsterdam corrupted his name (Saint Nicholas to Sint Klaes to Santa Claus), that he grew into his present role.

The people composed Christmas as an expression of religious devotion and secular pageantry. It is a work that has never ended; it proceeds as vigorously today as it did 1,000 years ago. Part One of THE GLORY AND PAGEANTRY OF CHRISTMAS re-created in text and fine art the ageless glory of the first Christmas.

The story of the people's creation of Christmas is the story of Part Two. In dealing with the development of Christmas pageantry, each chapter of Part Two begins with a quotation that sets the tone of what follows. Each chapter then describes and illustrates a particular period of history, with emphasis on its special contributions to the stream of traditions. Thus Chapter IX traces the beginnings of pageantry in the pagan past. It shows how the early Church Fathers, recognizing the superstitious and emotional attachment of the people to their pagan rites, sought to give them a Christian significance. Then follows an anthology of prose, poetry and music, in which the living voices of the era can be heard. The final chapter in this section offers photographic evidence that the synthesis of Christmas continues still.

Altogether, Part Two presents the evolving nature of Christmas, its unfolding and enrichment over the centuries. The world's great art museums and private libraries were searched for glimpses of many different kinds of Christmas: those of real people and legendary figures, of Charlemagne and King Arthur, St. Francis and Shakespeare, Martin Luther and Queen Victoria. All have become part of Christmas. So has the inventive 19th Century New York cartoonist, Thomas Nast, who first sketched the familiar Santa Claus of today.

Here are 20 centuries of glittering Christmas pageantry: parties, pagan rites, knightly tournaments, miracle plays, Lords of Misrule, Boy Bishops, boars' heads, peacock pies, plum puddings, Christmas carols, cards and trees. "The lifeblood of a people is its traditions," Dr. Count says. This section presents the traditions and the lustrous pageantry of Christmas.

—THE EDITORS

IX

THE EARLIEST YEARS

I HAVE, UPON MATURE DELIB-
eration on the affair of the English, determined upon, viz., that the
temples of the idols in that nation
ought not to be destroyed; but let the
idols that are in them be destroyed;
let holy water be made and sprinkled
in the said temples, let altars be
erected, and relics placed. For if
those temples are well built, it is
requisite that they be converted from
the worship of devils to the service of
the true God; that the nation, seeing
that their temples are not destroyed,
may remove error from their hearts,
and knowing and adoring the true
God, may the more familiarly resort
to the places to which they have been
accustomed. . . . For there is no doubt
that it is impossible to efface every
thing at once from their obdurate
minds; because he who endeavours
to ascend to the highest place, rises
by degrees or steps, and not by leaps.

POPE GREGORY'S LETTER TO AN ENGLISH MISSIONARY

THE MADONNA OF MERCY *dominates this
painting in the first church dedicated to
Mary, Santa Maria in Trastevere, Rome.*

TURNING
PAGAN RITES
TO THE
PRAISE OF GOD

A SECTION OF MARBLE SLAB *used to shut tombs is marked with the Greek letters "chi" and "rho," identifying the figure as Christ.*

"HOW WONDERFULLY acted Divine Providence that on the day that the Sun was born—Christ should be born." So said St. Cyprian, a Third Century Bishop of Carthage. He was referring to December 25, when the winter days begin to lengthen.

St. Cyprian was ahead of many early Christians. Until 350 A.D., when Pope Julius I proclaimed December 25 as the date of the Nativity, almost every month in the year had, at one time or another, been named by reputable scholars as the likely date of Christ's birth. There is still disagreement about the actual historical date, but for practical purposes Pope Julius' choice has long been accepted by all the churches except the Armenian, which still observes Christmas on January 6.

By the time of Pope Julius' proclamation, Christianity was on its way to becoming a world religion. Its establishment had taken more than 300 years. Eleven Apostles had set out to spread the teachings of their crucified Lord. They had traveled far—St. Peter to Rome; St. Thomas, tradition says, to India. A great organizer, St. Paul, knit the scattered Christian communities into a cohesive and flourishing church.

They and their converts had met sporadic, but always brutal, persecution from the Roman authorities. In 64 A.D. Peter and Paul had been killed when Nero made Christians the scapegoats for his burning of Rome. Worse waves of persecution had followed. In 303 A.D., Emperor Diocletian celebrated the Nativity by putting 20,000 Roman Christians to death by fire. Once again the faithful were driven into their underground tombs, the catacombs *(opposite)*.

But in 313, Emperor Constantine, himself a Christian convert, issued his Edict of Toleration, which legalized Christianity throughout the Roman Empire. And in 392 Theodosius I was to outlaw paganism. It was on this rising tide that Pope Julius declared December 25 the feast of the Nativity.

Christians, for whom Christ was the new beginning and the new light of the world, celebrated His birth in a seasonal tradition which crosscut a number of cultures. During the winter solstice, ancient Mesopotamians performed rites to aid their god Marduk in his struggle against the forces of chaos. At that season, the Greek Zeus began anew his battle against Kronos (Time) and the Titans. The followers of Mithras, a Persian sun-god whose cult was brought to Rome by returning legionaries and became the chief rival of Christianity, celebrated December 25 as *Dies Solis Invicti Nati* (Birthday of the Unconquered Sun). The Romans themselves had long celebrated the solstice season as the Saturnalia, honoring Saturn, the god of agriculture.

During Saturnalia, normal life turned upside down. Gambling was declared legal, courts were closed, and no one could be convicted of a crime. Slaves dressed in their masters' clothes and were served by their masters. A mock king was chosen to rule the festivities: He would turn up at Christmas again, centuries later, as the Lord of Misrule. Lavish holiday banquets featured such delicacies as peacock eggs in pepper sauce. The exchange of gifts became an important part of the festivities. They were simple at first—wax candles or clay dolls—but they slowly grew more elaborate.

Christians began absorbing these old customs and infusing them with Christian meaning in order to help spread the faith. Many Church fathers considered the method dangerous. St. Augustine, the greatest theologian of the Fourth Century, warned his people: "We hold this day holy, not like the pagans because of the birth of the sun, but because of Him who made it."

But most of the Christian missionaries who moved into Central and Western Europe as the Roman Empire crumbled, followed the advice of Gregory the Great. He wrote, in 597, that they should not try to put down pagan customs "upon the sudden," but adapt them "to the praise of God."

In the North, at the Christmas season, the missionaries found the pagan adherents of the gods Woden and Thor battling the winter's evil darkness with huge bonfires. In Central Europe, they found the belief that at the death of the old sun, witches and fiery demons came to earth to destroy the fertility of the new year, and could be dissuaded by presents. In Britain, they found Druids paying tribute to the victory of evergreens over winter's darkness.

The missionaries, heeding Gregory the Great's advice, made no effort to "cut off" the "evil customs." As a result, many of them survive as cherished Christmas traditions of today.

AN EARLY CHRISTIAN MOSAIC, *possibly the earliest known, decorates the ceilings and walls of a catacomb beneath St. Peter's Cathedral, near where St. Peter is said to be buried. The figure represents Christ but the symbol was previously used to portray a pagan sun-god. Such blendings of Hellenistic and Christian thought were common in the first years of the Christian Era.*

FROM UNDERGROUND TOMBS, A RENEWED FAITH

Of all the places where early Christians worshiped, none evokes a grimmer image than the catacombs. These enormous caverns, in some places five stories high, were built between the First and Fifth Centuries as cemeteries, located, by law, outside the city. When persecutions under the Roman emperors intensified, the Christians used the catacombs as places of refuge and prayer.

Paintings on the catacomb walls *(above and opposite)* indicate that the caverns had become real places of worship. Special services were held on the anniversary of a martyr's death, and special burial areas were set aside to the honor of various saints and martyrs.

The tombs made almost perfect refuges from persecution. Elaborate hiding places with secret openings

FOUR MAGI *bear gifts to Virgin and Child in this Fourth Century fresco from the Catacombs of Domitilla, Rome. The number of Wise Men varied in art works until the Sixth Century, when three became accepted.*

into adjoining quarries, blocked areas and false exits abounded. It has been estimated that more than 500 miles of galleries existed in the catacombs of Rome. Smaller ones harbored refugees in Sicily, Tuscany, Africa, Egypt and Asia Minor. One of the enduring legends of the Roman catacombs is that St. Peter preached in them and that he is buried in their endless labyrinth.

A CHRISTIAN WOMAN *lifts her arms in prayer in a Third Century fresco from the Roman Catacombs of Domitilla. In early Christian art, this figure, called an "orant," was used as a symbol of the faithful dead.*

117

THE BIRTH OF ST. NICHOLAS, *his call to God's service and his gifts to the three poor maidens are depicted (left to right) in this panel painted by Fra Angelico.*

ST. NICHOLAS OF BARI *saves a ship and greets an envoy (right). The Fra Angelico panels on these pages were painted for San Domenico Church, Perugia.*

THE SERENITY OF ST. LUCY *stands out in this detail from a mosaic illustrating a procession of virgin martyrs at Ravenna, Italy. Devotion to the devout and saintly girl goes back to the Fourth Century.*

SAINTS TO HONOR IN THE DAYS TO COME

Two of the early Christian saints are especially honored during the Christmas season—St. Nicholas on December 6 in Holland and St. Lucy on December 13 in Sweden.

St. Nicholas, a kindly Fourth Century bishop, is the patron saint of children, sailors, marriageable maidens and pawnbrokers. The last two roles are connected: Nicholas once gave three bags of gold as dowries for three daughters of a poor man; the bags, stylized as golden balls, became the pawnbroker's emblem.

St. Lucy, who died in 304, was a devout Sicilian girl who made a vow of chastity. Her rejected suitor denounced her as a Christian, and Diocletian's soldiers killed her. Her feast is celebrated with blazing candles.

THE DEATH OF ST. NICHOLAS *follows a scene showing him rescuing three condemned innocents. Many shrines were built in his honor in medieval England.*

THE ORIGIN OF SPECIES

The Fourth Century St. Nicholas was a modest man who did good deeds in secret. This poem by Phyllis McGinley points out how his popular image has been changed over the centuries.

Nicholas, Bishop of Myra's See,
Was holy a saint
As a saint could be;
Saved not a bit
Of his worldly wealth
And loved to commit
Good deeds by stealth.

Was there a poor man,
Wanting a roof?
Nicholas sheltered him weatherproof.
Who lacked a morsel
Had but to ask it
And at his doorsill
Was Nicholas' basket.

O, many a basket did he carry!
Penniless girls
Whom none would marry
Used to discover to their delight,
Into their windows
Tossed at night
(When the moon was old
And the dark was showery),
Bags of gold
Enough for a dowery.

People, I read,
Grew slightly lyrical,
Calling each deed
He did, a miracle.
Told how he calmed the sea for sailors

And rescued children
From awful jailors
Who, drawing lots
For the foul design,
Liked pickling tots
In pickle-brine.

Nicholas, *circa*
Fourth cent. A. D.,
Died in the odor of sanctity.
But fortune changes,
Blessings pass,
And look what's happened to Nicholas.

He who had feared
The world's applause,
Now, with a beard,
Is Santa Claus.
A multiplied elf, he struts and poses,
Ringing up sales
In putty noses;
With Comet and Cupid
His constant partners,
Telling tall tales to kindergart'ners,
His halo fickle as
Wind and wave.

While dizzily Nicholas
Spins in his grave.

St. Lucy's Plea

St. Lucy, a Fourth Century martyr who is honored at Christmas, dedicates herself to piety in this scene by Jacobus de Voragine (1230-1298).

"Mother, now thou art cured and healthy, I pray thee for my sake whose prayers healed thee, never to suggest to me that I take a husband nor spouse, but with the dowry that thou wouldst give me, I pray thee to give it to me for alms, so that I may come unto my savior Jesus Christ." Her mother answered, "Fair daughter I have not decreased thy patrimony which I received nine years ago when thy father died, but I have multiplied and increased it. But wait until I am departed out of this world and then do as it shall please thee." Lucy replies: "After thou art dead thou may not use thy goods. . . . Give them for God's sake while thee live, every day give of thy goods."

Hodie Christus Natus Est

"Hodie Christus Natus Est" ("This day Christ is Born") is a Gregorian chant of the Seventh Century which is sung at Vespers on Christmas Day.

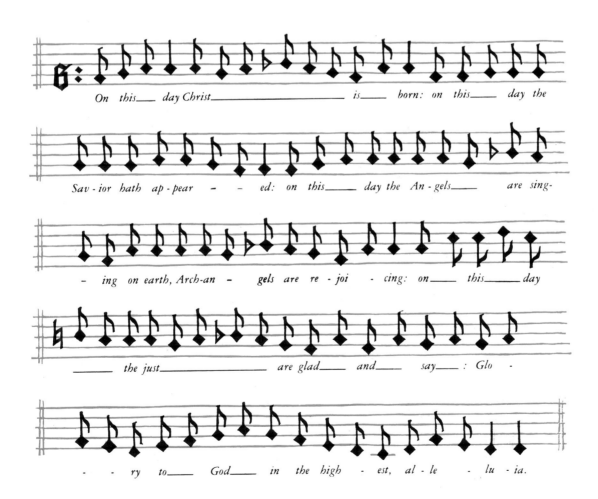

X

A MILITANT FAITH

HEAP ON MORE WOOD!—THE wind is chill; But let it whistle as it will, We'll keep our Christmas merry still. Each age has deemed the new-born year The fittest time for festal cheer: Even, heathen yet, the savage Dane, At Iol more deep the mead did drain; High on the beach his galleys drew, And feasted all his pirate crew; Then in his low and pine-built hall, Where shields and axes decked the wall, They gorged upon the half-dressed steer; Caroused in seas of sable beer; While round, in brutal jest, were thrown The half-gnawed rib, and marrow-bone; Or listened all, in grim delight, While scalds yelled out the joys of fight. Then forth, in frenzy, would they hie, While wildly loose their red locks fly, And, dancing round the blazing pile, They make such barbarous mirth the while, As best might to the mind recall The boisterous joys of Odin's hall.

"MARMION," SIR WALTER SCOTT

DEVOUT KING EDGAR, *shown flanked by Mary and St. Peter, offers Christ the charter of an English abbey he refounded in 966.*

RITES AND REVELS OF THE CONQUERORS

AN ANCIENT ROUND TABLE, *reputedly used by King Arthur and his knights, now hangs from a wall in England's Winchester Castle.*

DURING the early Middle Ages, roughly from the Fifth Century through the 11th Century, the celebration of Christmas was radically changed by the same mighty forces that were reshaping European history. Hordes of pagan warriors swept out of the North and East, occupying rich lands in their path. Meanwhile Christianity had grown from a missionary sect into a politically powerful institution. Its influence spread from the churches and monasteries into the strongholds of the conquerors. Increasing numbers of these rough fighting men were converted to the dynamic new faith. Their celebration of Christ's birthday mingled with their old pagan festivals held in December, when there was leisure between the fall harvest and the spring planting. Inevitably, many important state occasions were scheduled for Christmas, borrowing spiritual grandeur from the day and lending it crude pomp and gusto.

Few records survived the chaotic upheavals of the Fifth and Sixth Centuries, when Western Europe split into fragmentary kingdoms during the death throes of the Roman Empire. Yet as the war bands of the Angles and the Saxons overran England, there arose many legends cen-

tering on a heroic Briton who defended the Christian faith and his native soil from the invaders. He became known as King Arthur.

The myths of Arthur tell less about his age than about the ideals and attitudes that prevailed centuries later, when most of the stories were written. Probably the real Arthur was a rough captain of horsemen rather than the romantic monarch of resplendent knights. But, due largely to the *Morte d'Arthur,* the famous 15th Century epic by Sir Thomas Malory, Arthur and his Round Table became popular symbols of the whole medieval epoch.

Christmas is a portentous day in Arthurian legends. It was on Christmas Day that the miraculous event occurred which was to put young Arthur upon the vacant English throne. At the behest of Merlin the magician, the leaders of the realm gathered on the birthday of Jesus, in the hope that a sign from Him would reveal their rightful king. The sign took the form of a sword, embedded in an anvil, which only Arthur was able to withdraw. Malory also recorded (again with no support from history) that on a later Christmas, Arthur was crowned Emperor of Rome.

History records the long resistance of native Britons like Arthur, but the Anglo-Saxons ultimately established themselves in England. These Germanic peoples celebrated Christmas as lustily as their ancestors observed the pagan festivals of winter. For days on end, life was a boisterous round of singing, hunting, gambling, feasting and drinking wassail. Wassail bowls came into use; the beverage was usually ale or beer, sometimes hot and spiced, and it flowed in copious quantities. Alfred the Great, who reigned in the Ninth Century, tried

to curb the excesses. But the raucous revelry continued in spite of his pious decree that the 12 days after Christmas were to be set apart for sacred observance.

In the Ninth and Tenth Centuries, much of Europe fell to the Norsemen, or Vikings, from Scandinavia. Along with the Anglo-Saxons and the Franks and Goths, these fierce Norse sea lords accepted Christianity and retained in their Christmas celebrations several customs from their common pagan past. The ceremonial boar's head, which they served with its tusks replaced and an apple in its mouth, probably harks back to Frey, the Norse god of the herds, whose symbol was the boar. The blazing yule log, center of so many superstitions, remained popular, and so did the bonfires that had been lit on the shortest day of the year to speed the return of the life-giving sun. Another remnant was the use of evergreens. The Norsemen and Anglo-Saxons continued to decorate their halls with evergreen boughs during their Christmas revels, but as the generations passed they slowly forgot that the custom had been a pagan act in defiance of the winter's power to kill.

As the Norse conquerors weakened in England, another power was rising in France—the more advanced and worldly Normans. It was not until the Norman influence came to Britain that a genuine order and formality entered the English Yuletide festival. And it was on Christmas Day in 1066 that William the Conqueror assumed England's throne, firmly establishing the Norman line. For that great occasion, William organized festivities that were lavish beyond the dreams of his roughhewn predecessors. Thus began an elegant era in the celebration of Christmas.

THE KNIGHTS OF THE ROUND TABLE *welcome gallant Sir Galahad, who is being led by old Merlin the magician to the vacant seat between Sir Launcelot and King Arthur. By the 14th Century, when this illumination appeared in an Italian manuscript, the tradition had grown that Arthur and his knights spent their Christmas season in boisterous feasting and drinking.*

CLOVIS I, *King of the Franks, is baptized along with 3,000 of his men in a ceremony on Christmas Day in 496. The dove hovering near him symbolizes the Holy Spirit.*

CHARLEMAGNE *is crowned Emperor of the Romans by Pope Leo III on Christmas Day, 800. These illustrations are from a 14th Century French historical chronicle.*

A DAY FOR HISTORIC EVENTS

When the earliest of court Christmases were celebrated, kings were little more than warrior chieftains and their courts were drafty halls in rude fortresses. But Christmas had already become the great day of the year for holding affairs of state. In Saxon England, for example, the leading nobles of the realm gathered at Christmas to advise and counsel the king. These conferences, called the Witenagemot, were an early forerunner of the present-day British Parliament.

In this tradition, Christmas set the stage for three pivotal events of medieval history, all of them involving the close political relationship between Church and state. In the year 496, Clovis I, pagan king of the Franks, was baptized on Christmas Day in the first real step toward the formation of the French nation. His conversion gave the Church a powerful ally; and it won for Clovis the important political support of the bishops, which helped to make him master of most of Gaul. On Christmas Day in 800, Charlemagne was crowned Emperor of the Romans as a reward for defending the Pope against efforts to depose him. And on Christmas Day of 1066, William the Conqueror assumed the English throne with the Pope's sanction. In return, William shipped to the Pope generous Christmas gifts of plunder.

WITH BOAR'S HEAD AND WASSAIL BOWL, *a crude figure from a medieval English calendar personifies the pleasures of feasting and drinking during the court's Christmas celebrations.*

THE KING OF JERUSALEM, *Baldwin of Edessa, is crowned in Bethlehem, which the First Crusade freed.*

THE LEGACY OF THE CRUSADES

In 1095, Pope Urban called for a great crusade to end the Moslem persecution of Christian pilgrims in the Holy Land. With burning zeal, armies led by famous knights set out to free their sacred shrines. The First Crusade was a fierce struggle, but its warriors finally seized Jerusalem in July 1099, and they celebrated that Christmas in Bethlehem. There, on Christmas Day the next year, Baldwin of Edessa received the crown of the Latin Kingdom of Jerusalem *(above)*. Thus, 11 centuries after the birth of Christ, His Church returned to political power at the place of His birth.

Eight Crusades followed, each of them seeking to sustain the first. The survivors returned from the Holy Land with many treasures of art and literature whose influence was felt throughout Europe. And legends based on the Crusades, such as the story of St. George and the Dragon, found their way into early plays of the Christmas season, which have enriched its celebration ever since.

STORMING JERUSALEM, *knights of the First Crusade seize the city in 1099. This 14th Century miniature and the one above are from a French manuscript.*

129

Christmas with Arthur

Legend holds that King Arthur spent his Christmases in boisterous feasting and drinking. One such celebration is disapprovingly described in this account from an English chronicle of 1736.

At this time (A.D. 521) that great Monarch Arthur, with his Clergy, all his Nobility, and Soldiers, kept *Christmas* in *York*, whither resorted to him the prime Persons of the Neighbourhood, and spent the latter End of *December* in Mirth, Jollity, Drinking and the Vices that are too often the Consequence of them; so that the Representations of the old Heathenish Feasts dedicated to Saturn were here again revived; but the Number of Days they lasted were doubled and amongst the wealthier Sort trebled; during which Time they counted it almost a Sin to treat of any serious Matter. Gifts are sent mutually from and to one another; frequent invitations pass betwixt Friends, and domestick Offenders are not punished. Our Countrymen call this Jule-tide, substituting the name of *Julius Caesar* for that of *Saturn*. The Vulgar are yet persuaded that the Nativity of Christ is then celebrated, but mistakenly; for 'tis plain they imitate the Lasciviousness of *Bacchanalians*, rather than the memory of *Christ*, then, as they say, born.

OLAF THE KING

Christmas was officially observed in Norway for the first time by King Olaf in 995. In these verses by Henry Wadsworth Longfellow (1807-1882), Olaf and his Berserks, or armorless warriors, celebrate the day in their rough manner.

At Drontheim, Olaf the King
Heard the bells of Yule-tide ring,
  As he sat in his banquet hall,

Drinking the nut-brown ale,
With his bearded Berserks hale
  And tall.

O'er his drinking-horn, the sign
He made of the cross divine
  As he drank, and muttered his prayers,
But the Berserks evermore
Made the sign of the Hammer of Thor
  Over theirs.

Then King Olaf raised the hilt
Of iron, cross-shaped and gilt,
  And said, "Do not refuse;
Count well the gain and the loss,
Thor's hammer or Christ's cross:
  Choose!"

On the shining wall a vast
And shadowy cross was cast
  From the hilt of the lifted sword,
And in foaming cups of ale
The Berserks drank "Was-hael!
  To the Lord!"

THE BAPTISM OF CLOVIS

In the Middle Ages, Christmas was the traditional day for staging great state ceremonies. One such event—the baptism of Clovis I, King of the Franks, in 496—is described below in an account by St. Gregory of Tours (538-594).

Then the Queen [St. Clotilde] sent secretly to Rémy, Bishop of Reims, praying him to instil into her husband's heart the word of salvation. The Bishop came to the King, and little by little, and in private, brought him to acknowledge the true God, Maker of heaven and earth, and to renounce his idols, which could be of no avail to him or to anyone.

Then said Clovis to the Bishop: "Most holy Sir, I hear you willingly, but there is a difficulty: the people I rule have no desire to abandon their gods. Nevertheless I will speak to them according to the spirit of your words." He thereupon went into the midst of the people; but already the Divine grace had operated, and even before he opened his mouth to speak the assembly cried with one voice: "Pious King, we renounce our mortal gods, we are ready to serve the God whose immortality Rémy preaches." This news was brought to the Bishop, and overcome with joy he ordered the sacred fonts to be prepared. Rich hangings adorn the streets; the churches are hung with tapestries; the incense-clouds arise; fragrant tapers blaze on every hand; and all the baptistery is filled with a heavenly odour. Such grace did Almighty God shower upon those present, that they thought themselves transported among the joys of Paradise. The King first of all demanded baptism of the Bishop. Like a new Constantine he advances to the bath which is to wash away his deep-rooted leprosy, to the new water which is to cleanse him of the stains of his past. As he came to the font the saint of God addressed him with holy eloquence: "Bow thy head in humility, O Sicamber! adore what thou hast burned, burn what thou hast adored."

Clovis, having confessed one God, all-powerful in the Sacred Trinity, was baptised in the name of the Father, and of the Son, and of the Holy Ghost, and anointed with the sign of the Cross with the holy chrism. More than three thousand men of his army were baptised after him, as also his sister Albfledis, who a little time after departed this life in the Lord.

Boar's Head Carol

The boar's head feast was an ancient pagan rite that became a part of the Christmas season. This 16th Century carol, still sung in a yearly boar's head festival at Oxford University, England, captures some of the flavor of the rude times when the Anglo-Saxon kings reigned.

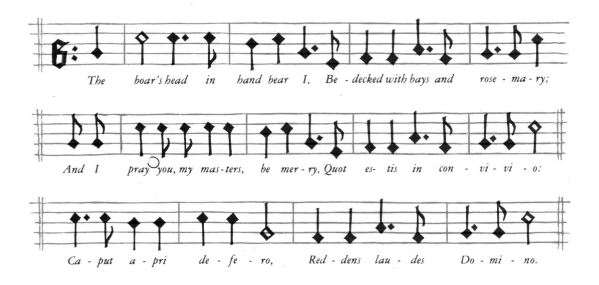

The boar's head in hand bear I, Be-decked with bays and rose-ma-ry;

And I pray you, my mas-ters, be mer-ry, Quot es-tis in con-vi-vi-o:

Ca-put a-pri de-fe-ro, Red-dens lau-des Do-mi-no.

XI
THE MEDIEVAL SPECTACLE

ST. NICHOLAS' DAY (DECEMBER 6) marked the opening of Christmas revelries. In the morning the Mayor and his fellows heard Mass and listened to a sermon by the Boy-Bishop; then, after dinner, they played solemnly at dice (a traditional part of the festival) until the Boy-Bishop arrived with a train of clerical attendants to give the town officers his blessing and be refreshed with bread and wine.... He was a busy man during this season dominated by the Lord of Misrule. The people of Bristol, like those of other towns, celebrated with mumming and gaming and dancing and brawls among visored rascals in dark streets. The Mayor heard sermons ... and on Christmas Eve he issued the usual proclamation against wearing of masks, carrying weapons, and remaining in the streets without lights after curfew.

"THE YORKIST AGE," PAUL MURRAY KENDALL

133

BESTOWING GIFTS, *the Duc de Berry (sitting at right) celebrates Christmastide amid lavishness typical of late medieval courts.*

AN AGE
OF FESTIVE
PAGEANTRY

AN EPIPHANY CAKE *is portioned out to guests in the order decided by the child tradition- ally called Phebe, sitting under the table.*

THE EPOCH called the late Middle Ages (roughly from 1100 to 1500) started with Christianity dominant throughout Western Europe. And it spread a wide variety of Christmas celebrations through all levels of medieval society. The Nativity was observed with simple, pious pageants and with impressive Masses in those glorious monuments which the age built to its faith—the Gothic cathedrals. But this was an age of vivid secular pageantry as well as piety, and Christmas was also celebrated with magnificent rituals of knightly combat, with fantastic pantomimes and garish processions, with organized horseplay and boisterous ringing songfests.

For kings and nobles, Christmas was a gorgeous season. In England their feasting was heroic. At Christmas 1252, Henry III had 600 oxen slaughtered. These were served with plentiful salmon pie and roast peacock, and washed down with barrels and barrels of wine. In 1415, Henry V observed Christmas with a "glutton mass celebration" that went on for five days. For his wedding to Katherine of France during the Christmas season of 1420-1421, the gigantic menu boasted pike stuffed

with herbs, jelly colored with columbine flowers, roast porpoise, smelt, crayfish and such obscure dainties as dedells in burneaux and frument with balien.

The wassail bowl of Saxon times maintained its prominent place in this trencherman's Christmas. In one recipe the basic ingredient, ale, was liberally spiked with sugar, apples, toast and roasted crabs. Topers intended no sacrilege when they implored:

> For our blyssd Lady sake,
> Bryng us in good ale!

Along with gourmandizing went lavish display in dress. For Christmas in 1201, King John of England "taxed his purse and ingenuity in providing all his servitors with costly apparel," and he was much vexed when the Archbishop of Canterbury tried to outshine him.

The giving of gifts —on New Year's Day and on Christmas—was customary by the 12th Century. Kings and nobles held to a scale of presents, usually money, for those in their retinue, but the gifts they exchanged themselves were often ostentatious. In 1236 England's Henry III received a truly spectacular present from the King of France —a live elephant.

Throughout the period, gaiety and excess increased. At Christmastime Spaniards danced in churches and Englishmen gambled with special fervor. Clerical warnings against these sinful acts had scant effect. In 1497-1498 English authorities settled for a forlorn victory by banning cardplaying by apprentices *except* at the Yuletide. Among many other Christmas extravaganzas were wrestling matches and grand hunting parties *(opposite)*. Foot and horse races were held on St. Staffan's Day, the

second day of Christmas, in Sweden, Germany and elsewhere. But for sheer spectacle none of the Christmas events matched the tournaments. In these contests, elaborately staged in many parts of Western Europe, knights matched lances before large, colorful holiday crowds.

In France, the special day for frolicking was Epiphany (January 6). It was the occasion for the Feast of Fools, a pagan survival in which certain members of the lower clergy elected their own Bishop of Fools. He conducted a mock mass, and "all sorts of buffooneries and abominations were permitted." Closely akin to the Bishop of Fools were England's Boy Bishops, whose religious satires took a milder form, and also the Lords of Misrule, who were appointed by noblemen and communities to lead their Christmas festivities. Official censure put a stop to the Bishop of Fools in the 15th Century, but the other festive figures continued to hold sway.

The French Epiphany was also celebrated with the *gâteau des rois,* or cake of the Kings. In one version of it, this big confection was baked with a single bean inside and distributed by the child called Phebe *(above)*. Whoever got the bean became the ruler of the day, chose a consort and ordered dancing and games. Apparently begun by monks in the 13th Century, the custom reached court circles and then ordinary homes, in some of which it is still observed.

By the end of the epoch, court Christmases could scarcely become more extravagant. Even the modest homes in England held elaborate festivities, while on the streets at night the minstrels and the poor and the mocking Lords of Misrule celebrated with roisterous merriment.

ON A CHRISTMAS HUNT, *spear-bearing nobles with their dogs pursue a boar (left) in this painting from an illuminated French manuscript of the 15th Century. The boar had been the symbol of a pagan deity centuries before. In later Christmas celebrations, the boar's head feast became associated with the court, and the boar hunt was a sport traditionally reserved for lords.*

PERFORMANCES TO GREET THE SEASON

POSING AS A BIBLICAL KING, *Charles VII of France is depicted presenting a gift to the Christ child in this Adoration scene painted by Jean Fouquet, a French court artist of the 15th Century.*

WEARING ANIMAL HEADS, *three mummers (below) cavort in this picture from a 14th Century manuscript. Such pantomimists also performed as dragons, peacocks and satyrlike wild men.*

Christmas in the late Middle Ages brought out a host of festive performers. By the mid-1100s, costumed maskers, or mummers, began appearing in the English court, where they acted out gay, fanciful pantomimes. Sometimes they dressed as animals *(left, below)* or as various fantastic creatures. The minstrels—a motley crew of actors, singers and jugglers—performed for coins in the taverns as well as the courts. To program all of their entertainments, kings and nobles often required their own special directors. These chief celebrants were called, appropriately, Lords of Misrule; and in a pagan tradition that dated to the Roman Saturnalia festival, they gleefully overturned the social order for the long Christmas season.

Even kings had their fling at festive masquerading. The occasion was Three Kings Day, which occurred on Epiphany, January 6. Celebrated in honor of the three Biblical Kings, this festival gradually became a major holiday in France and Spain. At Paris in 1378 three monarchs, including Charles V of France, attended Mass richly costumed as the Biblical Kings. A number of rulers posed for portraits in their disguise *(left)*.

The most important type of medieval performance was the drama. On the Continent, the only early drama was a simple, pious Christmas pageant which dramatized the birth of Jesus. It was variously known as the Nativity play, the miracle play, the mystery play. But in England another pageant, as simple as the Nativity play but more worldly in content, was also performed at Christmas. This was *St. George and the Dragon*, which dramatized the many legends of England's patron saint *(opposite)*. These representatives of two dramatic traditions, the religious and the secular, survived side by side for centuries, developing a store of dramatic knowledge that later contributed to the Elizabethan theater.

BATTLING THE DRAGON, *St. George (opposite) aims a deathblow in this 15th Century painting. The St. George legends grew up around a soldier who turned Christian and died as a martyr.*

De sancto georgio ā.   cepisset uenerunt ca pā
Cum autem beatus   docie regionis um excel
georgius in no   lentissimum et sanctum
mine dei marturium re   corpus eius nocturno

ENGLAND'S KING JOHN, *shunned as a despot, broods alone with his dogs. At Christmas 1214 he was served with demands that led to the Magna Charta.*

A TIME FOR TILTING AND CHIVALRY

The tournament, that public testing of knightly vows and valor, was the grandest of medieval displays; and many of the greatest tourneys were held at Christmastime. Richard the Lionhearted, brother of John (*above*) and a hero of the Age of Chivalry, was a flamboyant champion of the joust. One story tells that on Christmas Day, 1190, while he was leading the Third Crusade to a real war in the Holy Land, Richard paused in Sicily to stage a mock war. His powerful knights armed themselves with reeds, then joined the fray. To the victors Richard gave rich prizes.

Two centuries later, the second Richard of England presented a particularly dazzling Christmas tourney. Champions from all over Western Europe came to compete. On opening day, heralds and minstrels accompanied 65 steeds through London to the lists. Then came 60 elegant horsewomen, each one leading a knight in dramatic regalia. The warrior brotherhood splintered many a lance in their ritual of violence. After awards were made, the court returned to a sumptuous feast and a night of dancing. The whole lavish pageant was repeated daily for almost two weeks.

IN CEREMONIOUS COMBAT *before their fair ladies, knights clash with lances (left), while lesser men hurl spears and stones for distance. Such tourneys were the most spectacular of medieval Christmas events. The jousting riders shown above decorate a 15th Century chronicle.*

LOVE AND DEVOTION *bring St. Francis of Assisi into the fields to address the birds and the animals as his friends. This 14th Century stained-glass window is in a former monastery in Königsfelden, Switzerland.*

NEW MODES FOR MESSAGES OF FAITH

As the Middle Ages wore on, the celebration of Christmas moved slowly but steadily away from the Church. Miracle plays, which combined entertainment with moral lessons *(opposite)*, drew enthusiastic audiences. From the 14th Century on, the solemn Latin hymns of the Church were joined by music in a vivacious new style. In the new music, the melodies were based on dance rhythms and the words were sung in the native language of the land. They were carols from England, shepherds' songs from Germany and noels from France. They spoke of the personal side of the Nativity—the mother, the Babe, the animals and the love of God for His children.

These sentiments, too, moved St. Francis of Assisi, who loved all animals and often preached to the birds *(left)*. Seeking to bring home to people the joyful message of Christ's birth, the gentle friar built a life-sized crèche of the Nativity. The crib succeeded beyond his fondest hopes, winning wide popularity in his own time.

HORROR AND DROLLERY *are combined in this 15th Century illustration of a miracle play. It depicts graceful angels battling a band of weird devils for possession of the Castle of Faith.*

Cy commence le .v. et derrenier liure de ce present volume intitule / La for-
tresse de la foy .

vͤ et derrenier liure de ce present
volume experimenter quele chose
la force des dyables puet cͣ tre icel
le noſtre fortreſſe de la foy · Et ad
fin que ie puiſſe expliquer le cͣ
ceuement de ma penſee · xͥͥ · conſi
derations me viennent au deuant
en lentendement a traittier touchͣt

prez que nous
auons deͣoſtre
comment les bat
tailles des iuyfz
et des ſarrazins
gneſuent peu a
noſtre fortreſſe de la foy il reſte en ce

AN ELABORATE CRADLE, *probably used at Christmas to rock a figurine of the infant Jesus, is a 15th Century rarity from Germany.*

THE SPREAD OF HOLIDAY CUSTOMS

As medieval society grew more complex, the secular and the religious tended to merge in the celebration of Christmas. The crèche was often built in the town by lay organizations like the craft guilds; yet just as often the same groups, as parishioners, built the crib in the church. Carol singing, another of the age's original contributions to Christmas, was born in part as a reaction to the grave theology of Church music in Latin; yet in time these lively carols were also sung, in the vernacular, in monastery cloisters. Minstrels *(opposite)*, roving farther afield as travel grew safer and easier, made the same tunes favorites in many places. With the age's slow growth of commerce and its accelerating exchange of fresh ideas, no Christmas tradition died for the lack of exposure. In southern Germany the *Kindelwiegen (above)*, a cradle designed for a figurine of the Christ child, remained a local custom simply because it had limited appeal.

The new spirit which animated Christmastime heralded a new age —the Renaissance. In the Renaissance spirit of adventure an Italian captain sailing for Spain signaled the closing of the Middle Ages. And it was on Christmas Eve of 1492 that Columbus' cockleshell flagship ran aground on a reef in the New World.

A SCHOOL FOR MINSTRELS *rehearses before a teacher in this German illustration of the 14th Century. By then, such licensed vagabonds were spreading their gaiety throughout Europe.*

THE MISTAKE OF COLUMBUS

Marco Polo named Japan "Cipangu." When Columbus' ship ran aground in the New World on Christmas Eve, 1492, he believed he had found Japan. This excerpt is from his ship's log.

MONDAY: DECEMBER 24TH

Before sunrise, he weighed anchor with a land breeze. Among the many Indians who had come yesterday to the ship and who had indicated to them that there was gold in that island and had named the places where it was collected, he saw one who seemed to be better disposed and more attached to him, or who spoke to him with more pleasure. He flattered this man and asked him to go with him to show him the mines of gold. This Indian brought another, a friend or relation, with him, and among the other places which they named where gold was found, they spoke of Cipangu, which they call "Cibao," and they declared that there was a great quantity of gold there, and that the cacique carries banners of beaten gold, but that it is very far to the east. The admiral here says these words to the Sovereigns: "Your Highnesses may believe that in all the world there cannot be a people better or more gentle. Your Highnesses should feel great joy, because they will presently become Christians, and will be educated in the good customs of your realms, for there cannot be a better people or country. . . ."

The Dragon Killer

St. George, England's patron saint, lived in the Near East and never saw England. But in this passage from a medieval Christmas play he is called a Briton—and also a prince of Egypt.

Enter Father Christmas.
Here come I, old Father Christmas,
   Welcome, or welcome not,
I hope old Father Christmas
   Will never be forgot.
I am not come here to laugh or to jeer,
But for a pocketfull of money, and a skinfull of beer,
If you will not believe what I do say,

Come in the King of Egypt—clear the way.
Enter the King of Egypt.
Here I, the King of Egypt, boldly do appear,
St. George, St. George, walk in, my only son and heir.
Walk in, my son St. George, and boldly act thy part,
That all the people here may see thy wond'rous art.
Enter Saint George.
Here come I, St. George, from Britain did I spring,
I'll fight the Dragon bold, my wonders to begin.
I'll clip his wings, he shall not fly;
I'll cut him down, or else I die.
Enter the Dragon.
Who's he that seeks the Dragon's blood,
   And calls so angry, and so loud?
That English dog, will he before me stand?
I'll cut him down with my courageous hand.
With my long teeth, and scurvy jaw,
Of such I'd break up half a score,
And stay my stomach, till I'd more.

The Decline of the Joust

Christmas jousting kept the knights and their ladies in a gay mood. "The Shorter Cambridge Medieval History," in the paragraphs below, shows how the blood sport became relatively safe.

The typical sport of chivalry from the eleventh century, if not earlier in some form, was the mimic warfare of the tournament. The two main varieties, usually seen on the same occasion, were the joust or single combat with lance and sword, and the *mêlée* when two opposed parties fought. They were frequent and popular in the twelfth century; a skilful knight could support himself on the ransoms of those he vanquished. But the loss of life and limb in these murderous conflicts led the Church to condemn them under pain of excommunication of the participants. The Lateran Council of 1179 denied Christian burial to the slain. The effect, however, of these canons was small enough, although a steady tendency was shown from the thirteenth century towards lessening the danger by the use of blunted weapons. They gradually became more ceremonial and artificial. In the fifteenth century the *mêlée* almost disappeared, and the joust was mostly a test of skill in unhorsing an adversary with all precautions against collisions of the chargers and the like. Even so, sharp weapons might be used and men be killed outright. In Germany it was necessary for the jousters in these noble sports to prove ancestry unblemished by recent mésalliance. In general the tournament by these restrictions be-

came more and more divorced from actual warfare, but in fact in its cruder form it had already lost touch with the advance of military science. To counter the long-bow, indeed, the knight's armour had been much developed. Breast-plates and leg-armour of plate or leather had been added to chain mail, and the fifteenth-century complete suit of plate steel as well as the armoured horse were well in sight, but the result was cumbrous to a degree; the knight thrown to the ground was nearly helpless.

Coventry Carol

Nativity plays were often staged by medieval craft guilds. In 1534, the Shearmen and Tailors' Guild of Coventry incorporated this Christmas carol in their famous play.

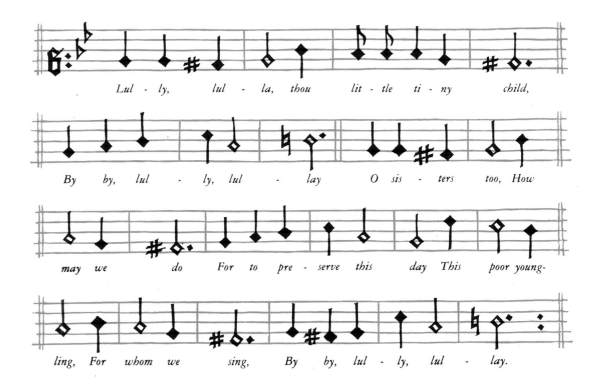

XII

IN AND OUT OF FAVOR

ALL THE...HARMELESSE SPORTS, with the merry Gambolls, dances and friscolls, which the toyling Plowswaine, and Labourer, once a yeare were wont to be recreated, and their spirits and hopes reviv'd for a whole twelve month, are now extinct and put out of use, in such a fashion as if they never had bin. Thus are the merry Lords of misrule, supprest by the mad Lords of bad rule at Westminster. And to roast a Surloyn of Beefe, to touch a Collar of Brawne, to bake a Pye, to put a plumb in the pottadge pot, to burne a great Candle, or to lay one blocke the more in the fire for your sake (Master *Christmas*) is enough to make a man to be suspected and taken for a Christian, for which he shall be apprehended for committing high Parliament-Treason...

"THE COMPLAINT OF CHRISTMAS," JOHN TAYLOR

A GAY TREE *is paraded in a German square. This 16th Century painting is one of the earliest to show the Christmas tree custom.*

A BRIGHT
SEASON
BANISHED

HENRY VIII OF ENGLAND, *renowned for his Christmastime feasting, is depicted in this miniature with his jester, Will Somers.*

LUSTY AND PROUD, Henry VIII ascended the throne of England in 1509. By then, explorer John Cabot had staked England's claim to a New World empire. Henry, the epitome of the Renaissance king, was alert to the promises of exploration and prodigious in his appetite for life. His court functions and Christmas celebrations had an assured majesty that outshone his predecessors'. Of Henry's Twelfth Night festival in 1512, a court historian wrote: "at night, the King with XI others, wer disguised after the maner of Italie, called a maske, a thing not seen afore in England." After the banquet, "maskers came in with six gentlemen disguised in silke, bearing staffe torches, and desired the ladies to daunce." This elegant caprice was a masked ball, a glittering addition to Christmas.

In their city homes or country manors, noblemen and gentry created their own magnificence. Many of them kept "a maker of Interludes" to compose the yearly entertainments. Most of them employed as director of their festivities a Master of Revels or—continuing an older and wilder tradition—a Lord of Misrule. The clergy still had their revels too—the upside-down days when a Boy Bishop ruled. But in 1541, Henry VIII banned Boy Bishops, and a few decades later, the Lords of Misrule began to fade.

By 1541, the Reformation had begun. Luther had founded his Church. John Calvin was establishing his Calvinist, or Presbyterian, Church in Geneva. And, in 1534, Henry VIII had assumed control of the Church in England. Luther, though a reformer, was no puritan. He enjoyed the festival of Christmas, adding to it hymns of his own and, according to legend, the Christmas tree. Although the legend is more generous than accurate, it was among Lutherans that the tree first became a Christmas tradition. The earliest written record of a fully decorated Christmas tree dates from 1605, when a citizen of Strasbourg wrote that "at Christmas they set up fir trees in the parlors . . . and hang upon them roses cut from many-colored paper, apples, wafers, gilt-sugar, sweets, etc."

In England the Reformation did not immediately alter Christmas. But Christmas was being considerably changed by the sophistication of the Renaissance. The old, pious Nativity plays, which seemed coarse and superstitious to the worldly Renaissance man, were steadily dwindling. By the end of the century, they were seldom performed in England, and a new drama, complex and humanistic, was in full flower.

At the court on Christmas of 1594, the new drama brought together its leading patron and playwright—Queen Elizabeth and William Shakespeare. As an actor, Shakespeare often performed for Elizabeth and his plays remained a popular court attraction after James I succeeded her. During James's second Christmas season as king in 1604-1605, seven of Shakespeare's plays and two of Ben Jonson's were performed. In that season too, the first great Christmas masque was seen: Jonson's *Masque of Blackness.* It was a splendid blend of masquerade and music, and Inigo Jones, the finest stage architect of the day, produced it magnificently. It cost £3,000.

Puritans were shocked by such extravagance, and also by Christmas itself, which seemed to them dangerously pagan. One Puritan angrily noted that "in Christmas tyme there is nothing else used but cardes, dice, tables, maskyng, mumming, bowling, and suche like fooleries." In 1642 the Puritans came to power in England, and under Oliver Cromwell the streets of London resounded to the town criers' shouts of "No Christmas! No Christmas!" Playhouses were shut; the day of feasting was turned into a fast. When Londoners decked their streets with greenery, the Lord Mayor had the boughs all burned. Citizens were expected to report to work as usual, and Parliament declared that on the day "commonly called Christmas, no observance shall be had, nor any solemnity used or exercised in churches in respect thereof."

This severe attitude toward Christmas prevailed in New England too. The Pilgrims, who had started building their Plymouth colony on Christmas Day in 1620, still shunned the holiday in favor of hard work. The Puritans in the Massachusetts Bay Colony were threatened with a five-shilling fine for "observing any such day as Christmas." Throughout Cromwell's government, planters in the American South continued to celebrate their courtly Christmas. But even after Cromwell's downfall brought Christmas back to England, the holiday retained its solemn tone in most of Puritan New England.

A SPIRITED COUPLE, *Queen Elizabeth and the Earl of Leicester leap in a lively and informal dance. Elizabeth's Christmas entertainments also included masked dances and pantomimes, and she ordered court productions of tragedies, comedies and historical chronicles. Actor William Shakespeare often performed in these plays. This 16th Century painting hangs in Penshurst Place.*

THE MAGICAL WORLD OF MASQUES

Dramatist Ben Jonson was the master of the new form of courtly theater, the masque, and in the reign of King James his entertainments were frequently produced on Twelfth Night. Inigo Jones, England's first great architect, staged and costumed Jonson's masques. The result was both intelligent allegory and sumptuous show. Court people and events in their lives were often represented and celebrated in these masques. The *Masque of Hymen,* which Jonson wrote in honor of the marriage of the 13-year-old daughter of the Lord Chamberlain to the 14-year-old Earl of Essex, was acted in the Christmas season of 1606. Declared one guest, "I think they hired and borrowed all the principal jewels and ropes of pearls both in Court or city." At the end of the great performance, the women in the cast chose partners from the audience and the men performers "gleaned out the Queen, the bride, and the greatest of the ladies." And then they all danced.

AN ORNATE STAGE-SET *for a Christmas masque represents the façade of a palace. This design by Inigo Jones was drawn for Ben Jonson's "Oberon." The masque was first performed in 1611.*

FANTASTIC ATTIRE *for characters in "Oberon" (above) demonstrates the splendor and imagination of a regal age. The sketches are by Inigo Jones.*

A WINGED SPRITE NAMED IRIS, *from Jonson's "Masque of Hymen," hovers airily in another of Jones's sketches. The stage was banked with artificial clouds from which dancers descended.*

A TWELFTH NIGHT FEAST *is merrily celebrated in this painting by the 17th Century Dutch artist, Jan Steen. The child wearing the crown became king of the holiday by finding the one bean in his Christmas cake. Steen often portrayed the lively pleasures of Holland's rising middle class.*

HAPPY CELEBRATIONS IN THE HOME

Christmas was celebrated in 17th Century homes with a liberality based on new wealth. The fine feasts and prosperous families pictured by the Dutch painter Jan Steen give evidence of the abundance enjoyed by Holland's middle classes. Elsewhere in Europe, colonial trade and home industry enlarged a new class whose interests were commercial and whose pleasures were domestic.

The stage for their celebrations was the home. The importance of children in the Christmas season was increasing. As the paintings shown here suggest, the young were often the center of festivities.

One of the family's most popular Twelfth Night festivities was the choosing of the King of the Bean. Traditionally, the bean was hidden in a cake; the finder became mon-

arch of the night, chose a queen and ordered the court to drink or dance. Since Twelfth Night concluded the season, it often produced marathon revels. On one such occasion, the English diarist Samuel Pepys saw the bean king chosen in his home, then recorded that he wearily retired, "leaving my wife and people at their sports, which they continued till morning, not coming to bed at all."

ST. NICHOLAS' GIFTS, *found in the shoes in this Dutch scene, delight a good girl and sadden the bad boy who got only a switch. The basket on the floor contains St. Nicholas' Eve cakes.*

A BAND OF CHERUBS *encircles this cast of a Christmas dough-mold from Germany. The center scene shows Jesus turning water into wine. Cakes were baked in such molds only on the holiday.*

SPECIAL HOLIDAY ARTISTRY

Christmas joy in the 17th Century was richly expressed in the ornaments and housewares that families brought out to welcome the glad season. Rooms were decorated with greenery and the walls were hung with bright tapestries like the Nor-wegian one shown on the opposite page. Traditional holiday foods were prepared. Cakes were made in ornate molds *(above)*. In France, Christmas cakes were formed in the shape of animals or men; a piece of the cake was said to be able to cure the sick.

In Scandinavia, Yule Boar bread was baked and some of it was set aside and mixed with seed in the belief it helped to make crops grow. Thus old customs combined with new festivities to make Christmas as cheerful at home as it was lavish in court.

A VARIETY OF COLORS *dramatizes the Adoration of the Magi in this brilliant 17th Century Norwegian tapestry. Hangings like this were used to bedeck the halls at Christmastime.*

SHAKESPEARE'S GIFT TO GOOD QUEEN BESS

In this excerpt from a story by Anna Benneson McMahan (1846-1919), a play by Shakespeare is presented at Christmas for Elizabeth I.

The numberless diamond-shaped window panes of the Mermaid Tavern are twinkling like so many stars in the chill December air of London. It is the last meeting of the Mermaid Club for the year 1596, and not a member is absent. As they drop in by twos and threes and gather in groups about the room, it is plain that expectation is on tip-toe. . . . Some are young, handsome, fastidious in person and dress; others are bohemian in costume, speech, and action; all wear knee breeches, and nearly all have pointed beards. He of the harsh fighting face, of the fine eye and coarse lip and the shaggy hair, whom they call Ben, although one of the youngest is yet plainly one of the leaders both for wit and for wisdom.

That grave and handsome gentleman whose lordly bearing and princely dress mark his high rank, is another favourite. He has written charming poems, has fought gallantly on many fields, has voyaged widely on many seas, has founded colonies in distant America, is a favourite of the Queen. But in this Mermaid Club his chief glory is that he is its founder and leader, the one whose magnetism and personal charm have summoned and cemented in friendship all these varied elements.

At last the all-important matter of the yearly Christmas play at court has been settled; the Master of the Revels has chosen from the rich stores of his manuscripts *The Midsummer Night's Dream*, graciously adding that "for wit and mirth it is like to please her Majesty exceedingly." A high honor, indeed, for its author. . . .

For now the successful candidate is one of the youngest and best beloved of this jolly coterie, and their pride in him is shown by the eagerness with which they await his coming to read to them the changes in the manuscript of his play since its former presentation. Ah! hear the burst of applause that greets his late arrival—a high-browed, sandy-haired man of thirty-two, lithe in figure, of middle height, with a smile of great sweetness, yet sad withal. On his face, one may read the lines of recent sorrow, and all know that he has returned but re-cently to London from the mournful errand which took him to his Stratford home—the burial of his dearly beloved and only son, Hamnet. The plaudits for the author of the most successful play of the season—*Romeo and Juliet* . . .—were little heeded by the grief-stricken father as he urged his horse over the rough roads of the four days' journey, arriving just too late for a parting word from dying lips. But private sorrows are not for those who are called to public duties; a writer must trim his pen not to his own mood, but to the mood of the hour. And Queen Elizabeth, old in years, but ever young in her love of fun and frolic and flattery, must be made to forget the heaviness of time and the infirmities of age. If she may no longer take part in outdoor sports—the hunting, the hawking, the bear-baiting—she still may command processions, fetes, masques, and stage-plays. It pleases her now to see this wonderful fairy piece, of which she has heard so much since, two years ago, it graced the nuptials of the Earl of Derby. Does she not remember also that pretty impromptu verse of the author when acting the part of King in another man's play, two years ago at Greenwich? Did she not twice drop her glove near his feet in crossing the stage? . . . And how happily had he responded to the challenge! True to the character as well as to the metre of his part, he had picked up the glove, presenting it to its owner with the words:—"And though now bent on this high embassy, Yet stoope we to take up our cousin's glove."

It is Christmas night. Lords, ladies, and ambassadors have been summoned to White-hall Palace to witness the play for which author, actors, and artists of many kinds have been working so industriously during the past few weeks. The Banqueting Hall, with a temporary stage at one end, has been converted into a fine auditorium.

Facing the stage, and beneath her canopy of state, sits Queen Elizabeth, in ruff and farthingale, her hair loaded with crowns and powdered with diamonds, while her sharp smile and keen glance take note of every incident. Nearest her person and evidently the chief favourite of the moment, is the man who has long been considered the Adonis of the Court. He is now also its hero, having but recently returned from the wars in Spain, where his gallantry and promptitude at Cadiz have won new glories for Her Majesty. In five short years more, his head will come to the block by decree of this same Majesty; but this no one can foresee and all voices now unite in praises for the brave and generous Essex.

nother conspicuous favourite is a blue-eyed, pink-cheeked young fellow of twenty-three, whose scarcely perceptible beard and moustache, and curly auburn hair falling over his shoulders and halfway to his waist, would suggest femininity except for his martial manner and tall figure. His resplendent attire is notable even in this gorgeously arrayed company. His white satin doublet has a broad collar, edged with lace and embroidered with silver thread; the white trunks and knee breeches are laced with gold; the sword belt, embroidered in red and gold, is decorated at intervals with white silk bows; purple garters, embroidered in silver thread, fasten the white stockings below the knee. As one of the handsomest of Elizabeth's courtiers, and also one of the most distinguished for birth, wealth, and wit, he would be a striking figure at any time; but tonight he has the added distinction of being the special friend and munificent patron of the author of the play that they have come to witness. To him had been dedicated the author's first appeal to the reading public—a poem called "Venus and Adonis," published some three years since; also, a certain "sugared sonnet," privately circulated, protesting—

> For to no other pass my verses tend
> Than of your graces and your gifts to tell.

And through the patronage of this man—the gracious Earl of Southampton—the actor-author was first brought to the Queen's notice, finally leading to the present distinction at her hands.

But now the stage compels attention. The silk curtains are withdrawn, disclosing a setting of such elaboration and illusion as never before has been witnessed by sixteenth century eyes. Never before has the frugal Elizabeth consented to such an expenditure for costumes, properties, lights, and music. In vain the audience awaits the coming of the author; he is behind the scenes, an anxious and watchful partner with the machinist in securing the proper working of these new mechanical appliances, and the smoothness of the scene shifting. The Queen is a connoisseur in these matters, and there must be no bungling. . . .

he Christmas play is over, but not over the Christmas fun. Lords and ladies are but human, and have devised a "stately dance," in which they themselves participate until nearly sunrise, the Queen herself joining at times, and never so happy as when assured of her "wondrous majesty and grace."

EVELYN'S ARREST

Cromwell's Puritan hatred of the "popery" of Christmas is vividly described below in a selection from the diary of John Evelyn (1620-1706).

25 I went to London with my Wife, to celebrate Christmas-day, Mr. Gunning preaching . . . as he was giving us ye Holy Sacrament, the chapell was surrounded with souldiers, and all the communicants and assembly surpriz'd and kept prisoners by them, some in the house, others carried away. It fell to my share to be confin'd to a roome in the house, where yet I was permitted to dine with the master of it, ye Countesse of Dorset, Lady Hatton, and some others of quality who invited me. In the afternoone came Col. Whaley, Goffe, and others, from White-hall, to examine us one by one. . . . When I came before them they tooke my name and abode, examin'd me why, contrary to an ordinance made that none should any longer observe ye superstitious time of the Nativity (so esteem'd by them), I durst offend, and particularly be at Common Prayers, which they told me was but ye masse in English, and particularly pray for Charles Steuart, for which we had no Scripture. I told them we did not pray for Cha. Steuart, but for all Christian Kings, Princes, and Governors. They replied, in so doing we praied for the K. of Spaine too, who was their enemie and a papist, with other frivolous and insnaring questions and much threatning; and finding no colour to detaine me, they dismiss'd me with much pitty of my ignorance. These were men of high flight and above ordinances, and spake spiteful things of our Lord's Nativity. As we went up to receive the Sacrament the miscreants held their muskets against us as if they would have shot us. . . .

Christmas with Pepys

A domestic Christmas in London, both devout and quietly festive, is described in this entry from the diary of Samuel Pepys (1633-1703). It is 1666, the year of the great London fire.

25 Christmas day Lay pretty long in bed, and then rose, leaving my wife desirous to sleep, having sat up till four this morning seeing her mayds make mince pies. I to church, where our parson Mills made a good sermon. Then home, and dined on some good ribbs of beef roasted and mince pies; only my wife, brother, and Barker, and plenty of good wine of my owne, and my heart full of true joy; and thanks to God Almighty for the goodness of my condition at this day. After dinner, I begun to teach my wife and Barker my song, "It is decreed," which pleases me mightily as now I have Mr. Hinxton's base. Then out and walked alone on foot to the Temple, it being a fine frost, thinking to have seen a play all alone; but there, missing of any bills, concluded there was none, and so back home; and there with my brother reducing the names of all my books to an alphabet, which kept us till 7 or 8 at night, and then to supper, W. Hewer with us, and pretty merry, and then to my chamber to enter this day's journal only. . . .

Christmas Banned

The Puritan ban on all Christmas celebrations was enforced in the New World by the Massachusetts Bay Colony in this decree reprinted from its legislative record of May 11, 1659.

For pventing disorders arising in seuerall places wthn this jurisdiccon, by reason of some still observing such ffestiualls as were superstitiously kept in other countrys, to the great dishonnor of God & offence of others, it is therefore ordered by this Court and the authority thereof, that whosoeuer shall be found observing any such day as Christmas or the like, either by forbearing of labour, feasting, or any other way, vpon any such accounts as aforesajd, euery such person so offending shall pay for euery such offence fiue shillings, as a find to the county. And whereas, not only at such tjmes, but at seuerall other tjmes also, it is a custome too frequent in many places to expend time in vnlawfull games, as cards, dice &c, it is therefore futher ordered, and by the Court declared, that, after publication hereof, whosoeuer shall be found in any place wthin this jurisdiccon playing either at cards or at dice, contrary to this order, shall pay as a fine to the county the some of fiue shillings for euy such offence.

TWELFTH NIGHT WITH FRANCIS

"The Gentleman of Renaissance France" contains this description of the wild court fêtes in France under King Francis I (1494-1547).

The King and his retinue, after having made a little sojourn at Amboise around Christmas, went on north a few miles to spend the *fête des Rois* (or Twelfth Night) of 1521 at Romorantin. It all started when the news came to Francis that the Comte de Saint-Pol in his house nearby had just chosen a king for the festival: some courtier had already by chance found in the Twelfth Night cake the large bean that made him king for the day, a gay ceremony that is still done in France on the sixth of January. The King, in high good spirits, decided "with the young gentlemen of his court" to challenge the authority of this king that had got his crown so easily. Saint-Pol and a group in his domain accepted the challenge, and laid in a supply of ammunition to defend the temporarily royal castle against the besiegers. The defense material consisted of a "prodigious quantity of snowballs, eggs, and apples," which turned out not to be enough to repel the assault, for the attackers were soon pushing in the doors and the ammunition was all gone. In the excitement, someone snatched a burning chunk of wood from a fireplace upstairs and threw it out a window. It struck the King on the side of the head, wounding him quite seriously. Nevertheless, he would permit no investigations to be made as to who had thrown the almost deadly missile, saying that if he indulged in such tomfoolery, he would have to take his chances on any accident. . . . It seems likely that the episode caused the King to have a permanent scar . . . which he covered with a beard—and thus popularized beards at Court.

INDIAN EPIPHANY

Father Jean Enjalran, a Jesuit missionary in Canada, reveals the childlike piety of many Indian converts in his 1679 account of an Epiphany celebration from the "Jesuit Relations."

All our savages, but especially the hurons, profess to have a special esteem for the all-endearing mystery of the birth of our lord Jesus Christ. I have seen some notable proofs of this given by these latter; they themselves entreated the father, long before the feast-day, to make arrangements so as to celebrate it in the most solemn manner possible. They sent their children to seek for what could be used in constructing a grotto, in which they were to make a representation of the mystery; and I took pleasure in hearing a little girl who, having brought with much care a beautiful sort of grass, said that she had done it in the thought and hope that the little infant Jesus might be Laid upon that grass. Our good Christians made some more serious preparations, For they all confessed; and those to whom permission was given to receive Communion, did

so very devoutly, at the midnight mass. The grotto, which was well fitted to inspire devotion, was Incessantly visited; and it rendered a very pleasing although rather protracted Service,—to draw from them the expression of their feelings as they themselves express them, when addressing the divine child. As a Climax to their devotion, they asked that the infant Jesus should do them the favor of visiting them, by being carried through their village. But, as they thought that they had rendered themselves Unworthy of this by some things that had taken place, they held grand Councils and took great precautions to obtain this favor from their missionary. The Matter was conceded to them, and carried out on the Day of the epiphany in a manner that seems to me worthy of being recorded. For my part, I was much touched by it.

They desired, then, in execution of their design, to imitate what in other ages had been done by the three great stranger Captains, who came to confess and adore Jesus Christ in the Manger, and afterward went to preach him in their own country. All the hurons, Christians and non-Christians, divided themselves into three companies, according to the different nations that constitute their village; and, after Choosing their Chiefs, one for each nation, they furnished them with porcelain, of which they were to make an offering to the infant Jesus. Every one adorned himself as handsomely as he could. The three Captains had each a scepter in his hand, to which was fastened the offering, and wore a gaudy head-dress in guise of a crown. Each company took up a different position. The signal for marching having been given them at the sound of the trumpet, they heeded the sound as that of a voice Inviting them to go to see and adore an infant God new-born. Just as the 1st company took up their march,—conducted by a star fastened to a large standard of the Color of Sky-blue, and having at the *rear* [head] their Captain, before whom was carried his banner,—The 2nd company, seeing the first marching, demanded of them [aloud] the object of their journey; and on learning it, they Joined themselves to them, having in like manner their chief at their head with his banner. The 3rd company, more advanced on the Road, did as the second; and, one after another, they continued their march, and entered our Church, the star remaining at the entrance. The 3 chiefs, having first prostrated themselves, and laid their Crowns and scepters at the feet of the infant Jesus in the Cradle, offered their Congratulations and presents to their savior. As they did so, they made a public protestation of the submission and obedience that they desired to render him; solicited faith for those who possessed it not, and protection for all their nation and for all that land; and, in conclusion, entreated him to approve that they should bring him into their village, of which they desired he should be the master. I was engaged in carrying the little statue of the divine infant, which inspired great devotion; I took it from the grotto, and from its cradle, and carried it on a fine linen cloth. Every one seemed touched, and Pressed forward in the crowd, to get a nearer view of the holy Child. Our hurons left the church in the same order in which they had come. I came after them, carrying the little statue, preceded by two frenchmen bearing a large standard, on which was represented the infant Jesus with his holy mother. All the algonquins—and especially the christians, who had been invited to assist in the pious function—followed, and accompanied the infant Jesus. They marched, then, in that order toward the village, Chanting the litanies of the virgin, and went into a Cabin of our hurons, where they had prepared for Jesus a lodging, as appropriate as they could make it. There they offered thanksgivings and prayers, in accordance with their devotion; and the divine child was conducted back to the church and replaced in the grotto. The Christian algonquins were afterward invited by the Christian hurons to a feast . . .

After this feast, at which, according to their Custom, the hurons did not eat, another and a special one was prepared for all the Christian and non-Christian hurons, spread by the officers in turn. This feast was preceded by a dance, as is their custom, whose sole object was that they might Rejoice together at the favor that they had received in the Visit which the new-born child had paid to their village. This dance is performed by the women only, as I said,—ranging themselves in two parallel lines at the two Sides of a Cabin, having in their hands a kind of Castanet. Those who are officers commence the Song and dance; they have some words to which they apply one of their airs, and these form the refrain of their Song which every one is to repeat to the same air. While the One who has Begun Goes on with her Song agreeably to the words which have served her for a refrain,— very often, however, varying the air,—she Runs and bustles about between these two ranks in a singular manner. In this there is nothing, as formerly, to violate decency, especially on occasions in which

they claim to honor God. Meanwhile the others—repeating at certain intervals the words which form the refrain, and which explain the intention of the one who is dancing—sound their Castanets, and move sometimes one foot, sometimes the other, to Certain measures without leaving their places. When some word which pleases them occurs in the Song they redouble the noise of their castanets.

OUR JOYFUL'ST FEAST

A former captain in the army of Cromwell, George Wither (1588-1667) might have been expected to disapprove of Christmas. Yet his "A Christmas Carol" is far from Puritanical.

So now is come our joyful'st feast;
Let every man be jolly.
Each room with ivy-leaves is dressed,
And every post with holly.
　　Though some churls at our mirth repine
　　Round your foreheads garlands twine,
　　Drown sorrow in a cup of wine,
And let us all be merry.

Now all our neighbours' chimneys smoke,
And Christmas blocks are burning;
The ovens they with baked meats choke,
And all their spits are turning.
　　Without the door let sorrow lie,
　　And if for cold it hap to die,
　　We'll bury 't in a Christmas pie,
And everymore be merry.

Now every lad is wondrous trim,
And no man minds his labour;
Our lasses have provided them
A bag-pipe and a tabor.
　　Young men, and maids, and girls and boys,

Give life to one another's joys,
And you anon shall by their noise
Perceive that they are merry.

Rank misers now do sparing shun,
Their hall of music soundeth,
And dogs thence with whole shoulders run,
So all things there aboundeth.
The country-folk themselves advance,
For crowdy-mutton's come out of France;
And Jack shall pipe, and Jill shall dance,
And all the town be merry. . . .

The wenches with their wassail bowls
About the streets are singing,

The boys are come to catch the owls,
The wild mare in is bringing.
Our kitchen-boy hath broke his box,
And to the dealing of the ox
Our honest neighbours come by flocks,
And here they will be merry. . . .

Then wherefore in these merry days
Should we, I pray, be duller?
No; let us sing our roundelays
To make our mirth the fuller.
And, whilst thus inspired we sing,
Let all the streets with echoes ring;
Woods, and hills, and everything,
Bear witness we are merry.

Huron Indian Carol

This Christmas carol, "Jesous Ahatonnia" ("Jesus Is Born"), was written for the Huron Indians in the Huron tongue by Father Jean de Brébeuf. Like the missionaries among the European pagans, he described the Nativity to the tribes in terms of their customs.

'Twas in the moon of winter time When all the birds had fled,
That migh-ty Git-chi Man-i-tou sent an-gel choirs in-stead;

Be-fore their light the stars grew dim, And wond'ring hun-ters heard the hymn:___

Je-sus your King is born, Je-sus is born! In ex-cel-sis glo-ri-a!

XIII
MANOR HOUSE HOLIDAY

HE AFTERWARDS FELL INTO AN account of the diversions which had passed in his house during the holidays, for Sir Roger, after the laudable custom of his ancestors, always keeps open house at Christmas. I learned from him that he had killed eight fat hogs for this season, that he had dealt about his chines very liberally amongst his neighbours, and that in particular he had sent a string of hogs' puddings with a pack of Cards to every poor family in the Parish. "I have often thought," says Sir Roger, "it happens very well that Christmas should fall out in the middle of the winter. It is the most dead, uncomfortable time of the year, when the poor people would suffer very much from their poverty and cold, if they had not good cheer, warm fires, and Christmas gambols to support them." "ESSAYS OF JOSEPH ADDISON"

POLITE SOCIETY *plays cards in a Hogarth painting. Card games and informality were the new Christmas mode in the 18th Century.*

A FREER, MORE SOCIAL CELEBRATION

A NOBLE OTHELLO *gestures on an Italian puppet stage. Marionette shows were at the peak of their vogue in the 18th Century.*

THE AUSTERE YEARS of the Puritan Commonwealth ended in 1660, and Christmas returned to England with the restoration of Catholic King Charles II. And like the monarchy, Christmas came back shorn of some of its old cavalier flamboyance. Its festivities became more social than ceremonial, more middle-class than regal. Its chief celebrants were no longer kings and nobles but the country squire and the rich merchant. No more aristocratic feasts of boar were carried in to the songs of minstrels or carolers, but a side of beef was served, or a pig, or turkey.

Besides this new informality, new humanitarian impulses entered the gentry's celebration of Christmas. An almanac of 1723, describing one squire's Christmas, remarked that he "invites his Tenants and Labourers, and with a good Sirloin of Roast Beef, and a few pitchers of nappy ale or beer, he wisheth them all a merry Christmas." After the meal, there would be dancing and songs, and often the night would end with ghost stories being told by the fire.

The squire often remembered the poor. One man's will in 1729 provided that each Christmas 20 pieces of beef should be doled out to those "such as had no relief on that day."

In the cities, the great masques of a previous age and the great silence of Puritan times were replaced by new forms of old public entertainment—the pantomime and the puppet play. John Rich, a London theater manager, introduced the Christmas pantomime to England in 1717, and his fantastic productions—with their Harlequins, Columbines, giants, fairies, fiends and dizzying plots—were a tremendous success. The puppet shows of the time were equally lavish. One, "Mr. Pinkethman's Pantheon," advertised fully 100 puppets and a show that "deserves to be esteemed the greatest wonder of the age."

Yet even more popular than such extravaganzas was card playing. No 18th Century Christmas was complete without it. Every squire got down his pack and every city party had its social game of whist or piquet. There were other games too, even less formal, that were played with gusto upstairs by the host and guests, and belowstairs by the servants: Blindman's Buff, Hot Cockles, Hunt the Slipper.

This genteel and social celebration survived, in America, among the Southern aristocracy. The country's first Christmas had been a Southern one when, in 1607, the Jamestown settlers had feasted and rejoiced in cavalier fashion. George Washington carried on this tradition. His Twelfth Night festivities of 1759, doubled in joy by his marriage that day to Martha Custis, were truly exuberant. A yule log blazed, firecrackers exploded, the halls were hung with green, and the party sat down to a generous feast. For Christmas, 1760—and for Christmases thereafter until the war —Washington, his bride and two stepchildren spent similarly gay holidays at Mount Vernon.

But America's Christmases were as varied as the peoples who had come to the new land. In general, Catholics, Episcopalians, Lutherans and the Dutch settlers rejoiced both in church and out, while Baptists, Presbyterians and Quakers tended to shun all observance of the holiday. In New England, an Irishman was chased out of town in 1755 when people discovered he was "a Christmas Man," but in Pennsylvania, one dour preacher noted, "Christmas & New Year holly days are seasons of wild mirth & disorder." In New York on December 5, the Dutch welcomed St. Nicholas, who visited homes and gave presents to the good and switches to the bad. In Missouri and Louisiana, French children put out their shoes for *le petit Noël* to fill, and in the Spanish Southwest, Mary and Joseph's long search for an inn was re-enacted.

Revolution, which strengthened the ties among America's many peoples, did not destroy their variety. Nor did America, in its revolt, utterly reject the traditions of its parent nation, England. It kept as much graciousness as it could afford, but felt no longer obliged to follow the fashions of any court. But the French, in their revolt, tried to destroy Christmas along with their monarchy. Church bells were melted for their bronze, worship was suspended on Christmas Day, and the *gâteau des rois,* or cake of the Kings, was renamed "the cake of Equality." By 1830, democracy had taken root in much of Europe, as it had in America, and the new Christmas was a democratic and all-inclusive one.

A CHRISTMAS PUPPET PLAY *in Venice is performed by figures a foot high. They include (from left to right) Brighella, Pantaloon, Harlequin, Columbine, The Lover and The Lady. Puppets were as popular in England during the Christmas season as they were in Italy. A London churchman complained that the puppet shows were packed but "we have a very thin house."*

ST. NICHOLAS' SINISTER HELPER, *Knecht Ruprecht, frightens children who do not know their prayers. He was also known as Black Peter.*

HOPES AND FEARS FROM THE PAGAN PAST

The Christmas season retained traces of old pagan fears as late as the 18th Century. To the superstitious the shift from the old year to the new was menacing—a time when good and evil hung in the balance. Knecht Ruprecht, the assistant to St. Nicholas shown in the German print above, was as capable of punishing as he was of rewarding, and the horns on his head reveal his demonic origin. Even St. Lucy, the patron saint of light, had her darker side; in the imagination of some Germanic folk she became the *Lutzelfrau,* a fearsome witch who rode the winds at Yuletide and who had to be bribed with little gifts. Perchta was another German Christmas witch. In south Germany, masked children, carrying brooms, went from house to house begging presents in her name. In other parts of Europe, the star-singers— a Dutch group is shown at the right in an 18th Century painting—roamed through the cities. They were welcomed for their songs and also for the blessing they were thought to give the house they stopped at. If they drew three crosses on a house, and the initials of the Kings, it was thought no harm would visit there.

STAR-SINGERS, *children dressed as the Three Kings and carrying star-shaped paper lanterns, sing carols to a family on Twelfth Night, while one boy reaches out for a gift. These costumed Christmas singers, once common throughout Europe, went from door to door, presenting pageants.*

Oh, I wish that coach were mine.

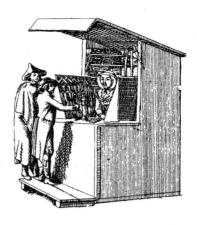

Let me look at that knife.

Here's money for that pair of pliers.

I would like some of those blocks.

What is it, boy? Just tell me.

Now then, what do you want?

I wanted a smaller lamp.

I have some splendid things, madam.

What do you want, little mouse?

I'd like an angel like that one.

Yes, that's the wagon I want.

These marbles are what I'd really like.

A FEAST OF LOVE *is observed by Moravians, a Germanic Protestant sect, with a simple meal of buns and coffee. This American print points out the pastor (A), the boys (B) and girls (C), and the servers (D and E). Moravian settlers celebrated the love feast in the U.S. as early as 1753.*

A TIME OF ABUNDANCE AND SHARING

By the 18th Century, the great Christmas fair in Nuremberg, Germany, was centuries old. But it still began, as in earliest days, in the first week of December, and at its opening a child dressed as an angel welcomed visitors. Hundreds of booths filled the square. Among their wares were the seasonal *Lebkuchen,* or ginger cake, as well as figurines of the infant Jesus. These were given as presents, continuing the Nurembergers' medieval tradition of "giving away the Christ child."

This affectionate generosity was also basic to the love feast which Moravians celebrated with Scripture, food and music. The Moravians, an early sect of Germanic Protestants, migrated to America in the 18th Century. Their love feasts continued in their new homeland, and so did their gifts of love. On Christmas 1760, it is recorded, Moravians in Bethabara, North Carolina, brought to their English neighbors a "pretty Christmas verse and a gingercake."

AN ARRAY OF BOOTHS *is open at the old Nuremberg Christmas market. The 12 shown in these German prints (opposite) display a variety of wares ranging from wooden angels to oil lanterns.*

High Life below Stairs.

A GAY SWIRL OF SERVANTS *celebrates Christmas in a room decked with holly and mistletoe. In this satiric English print by Robert Cruikshank, a three-man band (left) provides music for dancing, flirting or, as in the case of the man at far right, simply collapsing at three in the morning.*

NEW JOYS AND FREEDOMS

The democratic spirit, vigorous in America and in Europe in the late 18th Century, brought with it new attitudes toward the celebration of Christmas as well as a new freedom for all classes *(above)*. The opulent entertainments of the courts became increasingly discreet, and the organized anarchy devised by Lords of Misrule for the upper classes dwindled to parlor games. In America, the mummers' shows reflected the chang-

ing times: the old battle between St. George and the Dragon was being presented as a fight between George Washington and Oliver Cromwell.

In England, pantomime arrived on the stage. Actors in the legitimate theater looked down on this vastly popular entertainment. The satirical poet Alexander Pope scorned pantomime as a coarse show that "Dullness and her sons admire," and he described its usual plot as: "A fire,

a jig, a battle, and a ball, / Till one wide conflagration swallows all."

The new spectacles, numerous and popular as they were, formed but a small part of the typical Christmas. In the city a man's home, rather than the theater or the court, was now the main scene of celebration. And in the country the squire celebrated with decorum, offering food, drinks for all, a dance—and even a visit to church on Christmas Day.

A NEW CAST OF CHARACTERS *for a Twelfth Night pantomime is presented in this chart of punning riddles. These fantasies were the most popular stage events of the English Christmas.*

Park's New Twelfth-Night Characters.

KING OF HEARTS.

1. When is a king not a king?

QUEEN OF HEARTS.

2. Why does her Majesty resemble St. Swithin?

DICKY DAGGERWOOD.

3. Why is a melancholy young lady the pleasantest of all companions?

MRS. DAGGERANDO.

4. What description of drinking glass is more droll than others?

LORD BANDASH.

5. Why should a thin man make a better barge than a fat man?

LADY BOW-WELL.

6. If a single burner be taken from a chandelier, why should it be brighter?

SIR BENJAMIN BOUNCE.

7. Why are the first rays of the morning like an infuriated bull?

COUNTESS FLY AWAY.

8. Why is being cheated like a cockney lover's parting word?

SWELLERANDO.

9. Why is a man who beats his wife like a drunkard?

LADY LOW SLEEVE.

10. Why is a sick young lady like anything thrown from the hand?

LORD DUMBLE DUM DEARY.

11. Why is the chariot of Venus like the discoverer of the last planet?

LADY LOVEWELL.

12. Why are lover's sighs like long stockings?

LORD FLIRT AWAY.

13. Why is a statue like a fig?

LADY RAMBLE.

14. Why is a little demon sitting on a pent-house like a poor man?

SAMUEL SPRUCE.

15. When is leather like rust?

LADY LANGUISH.

16. Why are comic songs like gross blunders?

SPANTU LONG TONG SONG.

17. When is a blacksmith a hermit?

SING LING TING.

18. Why is 4s. 9d. a week, a government allowance?

LORD LOLLYPOP.

19. Why is a wife like a joint of pork?

MRS. STRUT.

20. When is a sailor above his commander?

SIR CHARLES C-GAR-UM.

21. Why does a carpenter live on addition?

LADY WARBLE.

22. Why is a monkey like an artist?

DAVID BANDASH.

23. When is Lent not Lent?

MADAME MANDOLINE.

24. Why is a baker like a grave digger?

LADY DASHALL.

25. Why does a printer dislike pastry?

LORD DASHAWAY.

26. Why is an unbound book like a young maiden in bed?

GEORGIE GALLOPPARA.

27. Why is a coxcomb like a law volume?

FANNY FANDANGO.

28. Why are butchers the strongest men in creation.

KEY TO THE CONUNDRUMS.

1. When he is a king-dumb (kingdom)
2. Because she always reigns.
3. Because she is always a-musing.
4. That which is called a *rummer*.
5. Because he's *lighter*.
6. Because its lighter by a lamp.
7. Because its a-roarer (aurora).
8. Because its *a-do* (adieu.)
9. Because he's addicted to lick-her, liquor.)
10. Because it is a missile (miss-ill)
11. Because it's her shell (Herschel).
12. Because they are heigh-ohs! (highlows).
13. Because it is an F I G (effigy).
14. Because he is an *imp-over-a-shed* (impoverished).
15. When it is ox-hide (oxide).
16. Because they are absurd ditties. (absurdities)
17. When he is an anchor-wright. (anchorite)
18. Because its under the crown.
19. Because she's a *spare rib*.
20. When he's mastheaded.
21. Because he lives by the *odze*.
22. Because he imitates nature.
23. When it is religiously KEPT.
24. Because he deals in dead men.
25. Because he is not fond of *pye*.
26. Because she's done up in *sheets*.
27. Because he's bound in calf.
28. Because they have more joints.

PRINTED AND PUBLISHED BY A. PARK, No. 47, LEONARD STREET, FINSBURY.

THE SQUIRE'S BANQUET

"The Sketch Book of Geoffrey Crayon, Gent." by Washington Irving (1783-1859) presents a classic description of Christmas in the English manor house tradition. In this excerpt from the book, the squire's Christmas dinner is bountiful but the aristocratic fare of earlier times is absent. A pig's head and pheasant pie replace the traditional boar's head and peacock pie.

The dinner was served up in the great hall, where the squire always held his Christmas banquet. A blazing crackling fire of logs had been heaped on to warm the spacious apartment, and the flame went sparkling and wreathing up the wide-mouthed chimney. . . .

We were ushered into this banquetting scene with the sound of minstrelsy; the old harper being seated on a stool beside the fireplace, and twanging the roast beef of old England, with a vast deal more power than melody. Never did Christmas board display a more goodly and gracious assemblage of countenances; those who were not handsome were, at least, happy; and happiness is a rare improver of your hard-favoured visage. The parson said grace, which was not a short familiar one, such as is commonly addressed to the deity, in these unceremonious days; but a long, courtly, well-worded one, of the ancient school. There was now a pause, as if something was expected, when suddenly the Butler entered the hall, with some degree of bustle; he was attended by a servant on each side with a large wax light, and bore a silver dish, on which was an enormous pig's head, decorated with rosemary, with a lemon in its mouth, which was placed with great formality at the head of the table. The moment this pageant made its appearance, the harper struck up a flourish; at the conclusion of which the young Oxonian, on receiving a hint from the squire, gave, with an air of the most comic gravity, an old carol, the first verse of which was as follows:

Caput apri defero
Reddens laudes Domino.
The boar's head in hand bring I,
With garlands gay and rosemary.
I pray you all synge merily,
Qui estis in convivio . . .

When the cloth was removed, the butler brought in a huge silver vessel of rare and curious workmanship, which he placed before the squire. Its appearance was hailed with acclamation; being the Wassail Bowl, so renowned in Christmas festivity. The contents had been prepared by the squire himself, being a beverage on the skilful mixture of which he particularly prided himself; alleging that it was too abstruse and complex for the comprehension of an ordinary servant. It was a potation, indeed, that might well make the heart of a toper leap within him; consisting of the richest and raciest wines, highly spiced and sweetened, with roasted apples bobbing about the surface.

The old gentleman's whole countenance beamed with a serene look of in-dwelling delight, as he stirred this mighty bowl. Having raised it to his lips, with a hearty wish of a merry Christmas to all present, he sent it brimming round the board, for every one to follow his example according to the primitive custom; pronouncing it "the ancient fountain of good fellowship, where all hearts met together." . . .

After the dinner table was removed, the hall was given up to the younger members of the family, who, prompted to all kind of noisy mirth by the Oxonian and Master Simon, made its old walls ring with their merriment, as they played at romping games. I delight in witnessing the gambols of children, and particularly at this happy holiday-season, and could not help stealing out of the drawing room on hearing one of their peals of laughter. . . .

The door suddenly flew open, and a whimsical train came trooping into the room, that might almost have been mistaken for the breaking up of the court of Fairy. That indefatigable spirit, Master Simon, in the faithful discharge of his duties as lord of misrule, had conceived the idea of a Christmas mummery, or masqueing; and having called in to his assistance the Oxonian and the young officer, who were equally ripe for any thing that should occasion romping and merriment, they had carried it into instant effect. The old housekeeper had been consulted; the antique clothes presses and wardrobes rummaged and made to yield up the reliques of finery that had not seen the light for several generations; the younger part of the company had been privately convened from the parlour and hall, and the whole had been bedizzened out, into a burlesque imitation of an antique masque.

Master Simon led the van as "ancient Christmas," quaintly apparel'd in short cloak and ruff, and a hat that might have served for a village steeple, from under which, his nose curved boldly forth, with a frost bitten bloom that seemed the very trophy of a December blast. He was accompanied by the blue eyed romp, dished up as "Dame mince pie," in the venerable magnificence of faded brocade, long stomacher, peaked hat, and high heeled shoes. The young officer figured in genuine Kendal Green as Robin Hood; the fair Julia in a pretty rustic dress as Maid Marian. The rest of the train had been metamorphosed in various ways; the girls trussed up in the finery of their great grandmothers, and the striplings bewhiskered with burnt cork, and fantastically arrayed to support the characters of Roast Beef, Plum Porridge, and other worthies celebrated in ancient masqueings. The whole was under the control of the Oxonian, in the appropriate character of Misrule . . .

It was inspiring to see wild-eyed frolick and warm-hearted hospitality breaking out from among the chills and glooms of winter, and old age throwing off its apathy, and catching once more the freshness of youthful enjoyment. I felt an interest in the scene, also, from the consideration that these fleeting customs were posting fast into oblivion; and that this was, perhaps, the only family in England in which the whole of them were still punctiliously observed. There was a quaintness, too, mingled with all this revelry, that gave it a peculiar zest: it was suited to the time and place; and as the old manor house almost reeled with mirth and wassail, it seemed echoing back the joviality of long-departed years.

Dreams of Grandeur

At Christmas Eve of 1811, Napoleon had Europe at his mercy. His military power is contrasted with the gentle spirit of the holiday in this fanciful scene from "Imperial Christmas."

It is Christmas eve of the year 1811, and Napoleon has been working alone in his office at the palace of the Tuileries since 10 o'clock in the evening. The large room is almost entirely dark. Here and there, in the shadow, shine some gilded objects, such as the frame of a picture, the heads of lions adorning the arms of a chair, and the heavy tassel of a curtain. Under their shades of metal, the wax candles of the two candelabra light only the large table incumbered with atlases and thick books bound in green morocco and stamped with the "N" and the crown.

The master has been working for nearly two hours, and on the geographical maps and on the charts marking the situation of his armies he bends his formidable forehead—that forehead heavy with thoughts, heavy as the world of which he meditates the conquest.

He has already the greatness of Cæsar and Charlemagne; he also wishes that of Alexander. He dreams this dream without wondering at it. He knows already the Orient; he has left behind him there an immortal legend. The Nile saw him one day, a thin general with long hair, mounted on a dromedary. On the banks of the Ganges the heavy Emperor, in his gray redingote, will need the elephant of Porus. He knows how to lead the people and how to fanaticize them. He will command soldiers over there with bronze faces, wearing turbans of white muslin; he will see mixed with his staff rajahs sparkling with jewels, and he will consult the monstrous idols, raising their 10 arms above their mitre of diamonds, about his destiny; since not long ago, in Egypt, the flat-nosed Sphinx, before which he dreamed, leaning on his saber, would not betray its secret . . .

But suddenly he raises his head with a movement of surprise. In his office, tightly closed and of which the heavy curtains are lowered, whence comes that strange and profound murmur? It seems as if the large gold bees embroidered on the silk hangings all begin to hum. The Emperor listens more attentively, and in that noise he distinguishes vibrations of brass.

"Ah! yes—Christmas—the midnight mass." . . .

The Emperor dreams—and in the confused sound of the bells which call to the midnight Mass he imagines he hears the cadenced march of the troops and the rolling of the ammunition wagons far away on the icy roads of Germany and Poland. Intoxicated with paternal ambition, he thinks more than ever of the Grand Army and of the conquest of Russia and India, and he swears to himself to leave to his heir all the thrones of the Old World. He has already given to him the city of St. Peter for a toy; the new-born will soon have other holy cities among his playthings . . .

And while the Emperor pursues his monstrous chimera, imagining the reign of his son and of his son's successors on the entire world, and fancying himself, Napoleon, having become, in the course of time and of legend, a fabulous myth, a new Mars, a solar god triumphant in the midst of the Zodiac of his 12 marshals, the bells still ring, joyously, triumphantly, desperately, in honor of the poor little Child born at Bethlehem, who really conquered the world 1,900 years ago, not with blood and with victories, but with the word of peace and of love, and who shall reign over souls in the endless chain of centuries.

CHRISTMAS WITH LEWIS AND CLARK

Two Christmases in the wilderness, in 1804 and 1805, are described by explorers Meriwether Lewis and William Clark in journal entries.

Tuesday, 25th December 1804. We were awakened before day by a discharge of three platoons from the party. We had told the Indians not to visit us as it was one of our great medicine days, so that the men remained at home and amused themselves various ways, particularly with dancing, in which they take great pleasure. The American flag was hoisted for the first time in the fort; the best provisions we had were brought out, and this, with a little brandy, enabled them to pass the day in great festivity. Wednesday, 25th December 1805. We were awakened at daylight by a discharge of firearms, which was followed by a song from the men, as a compliment to us on the return of Christmas, which we have always been accustomed to observe as a day of rejoicing. After breakfast we divided our remaining stock of tobacco, which amounted to twelve carrots, into two parts; one of which we distributed among such of the party as made use of it; making a present of a handkerchief to the others. The remainder of the day was passed in good spirits, though there was nothing in our situation to excite much gayety.

A GOOD GAME OF WHIST

♣ ♦ ♠ ♥

As Christmas became more domestic, cards became increasingly popular as a holiday diversion. Here is a portrait of a dedicated whist player, from an essay by Charles Lamb (1775-1834).

"A clear fire, a clean hearth, and the rigour of the game." This was the celebrated *wish* of old Sarah Battle (now with God), who, next to her devotions, loved a good game of whist. She was none of your lukewarm gamesters, your half-and-half players, who have no objection to take a hand, if you want one to make up a rubber; who affirm that they have no pleasure in winning; that they like to win one game and lose another; that they can while away an hour very agreeably at a card-table, but are indifferent whether they play or no; and will desire an adversary, who has slipped a wrong card, to take it up and play another. These insufferable triflers are the curse of a table. One of these flies will spoil a whole pot. Of such it may be said that they do not play at cards, but only play at playing at them.

Sarah Battle was none of that breed. She detested them, as I do, from her heart and soul, and would not, save upon a striking emergency, willingly seat herself at the same table with them. She loved a thorough-paced partner, a determined enemy. She took, and gave, no concessions. She hated favours. She never made a revoke, nor ever passed it over in her adversary without exacting the utmost forfeiture. She fought a good fight: cut and thrust. She held not her good sword (her cards) "like a dancer." She sate bolt upright; and neither showed you her cards, nor desired to see yours. All people have their blind side—their superstitions; and I have heard her declare, under the rose, that hearts was her favourite suit. . .

Quadrille, she has often told me, was her first love; but whist had engaged her maturer esteem. The former, she said, was showy and specious, and likely to allure young persons. The uncertainty and quick shifting of partners—a thing which the constancy of whist abhors; the dazzling supremacy and regal investiture of Spadille—absurd, as she justly observed, in the pure aristocracy of whist, where his crown and garter gave him no proper power above his brother-nobility of the Aces;—the giddy vanity, so taking to the inexperienced, of playing alone; above all, the overpowering attractions of a *Sans Prendre Vole,*—to the triumph of which there is certainly nothing parallel or approaching, in the contingencies of whist;—all these, she would say, make quadrille a game of captivation to the young and enthusiastic. But whist was the *solider* game: that was her word. It was a long meal; not, like quadrille, a feast of snatches . . .

Masters in This Hall

The verses of this Christmas carol were composed by the English poet William Morris around 1860. Its music, a traditional French air, embodies the vigorous rhythms of 15th Century carols sung in colorful processions to church.

XIV

THE VICTORIAN CHRISTMAS

THE CHRISTMAS TREE IS ANNUALLY prepared by her Majesty's command for the Royal children. . . . The tree employed for this festive purpose is a young fir of about eight feet high, and has six tiers of branches. On each tier, or branch, are arranged a dozen wax tapers. Pendant from the branches are elegant trays, baskets, *bonbonnières,* and other receptacles for sweetmeats of the most varied and expensive kind; and of all forms, colours, and degrees of beauty. Fancy cakes, gilt gingerbread and eggs filled with sweetmeats, are also suspended by variously-coloured ribbons from the branches. The tree, which stands upon a table covered with white damask, is supported at the root by piles of sweets of a larger kind, and by toys and dolls of all descriptions, suited to the youthful fancy. . . . On the summit of the tree stands the small figure of an angel, with outstretched wings, holding in each hand a wreath. "THE ILLUSTRATED LONDON NEWS," 1848

A TIMEWORN MEMENTO, *this elaborate Christmas card dates from Victoria's happy reign, when the greeting cards first appeared.*

FINALLY, CHRISTMAS REACHES OUT TO ALL HOMES

A VICTORIAN TIPPLER *sniffs his Christmas wine with delight. Many 19th Century recipes mixed wine and ale in wassail bowls.*

CHRISTMAS exuded middle-class cheer in the age of Victoria, the 64 years (1837-1901) in which the rotund little queen presided over the British Empire and the British Empire more or less presided over the world. In urban areas of America and Europe as well as in England, December stirred up a great hustle and bustle of ordinary folk to prepare for a more bountiful holiday. Improved roads and rails carried increasing numbers of people home for Christmas. Stores sold an ever-greater volume and variety of goods at Christmas. With the start of England's penny post in 1839, Christmas cards appeared; fancy and colorful, they soon spread across two continents, adding their cheerful bit to the general air of holiday well-being. Kindly, content and optimistic, Victorians recast the traditional figure of Father Christmas in their own image, transforming St. Nicholas, the formidable judge of childrens' behavior, into the merry, open-handed gift-giver called Santa Claus.

The queen, who heartily endorsed this more prosperous Christmas, much resembled its chief beneficiaries. Victoria, said a faithful historian of her time, "was possessed in high degree of queenly instincts and dignity, but they were softened and popularized by a mind and emotional nature of great simplicity. In herself she was not very different from her female subjects in humble stations of life."

Victoria's own Christmases typified the middle-class celebration of the holiday. The queen loved her hearth and children; she and her husband, the German Prince Albert of Saxe-Coburg, seldom left home for public festivities. She loved her candlelit Christmas trees with their gingerbread decorations, and she was proud that Albert had done so much to make the German tree custom an institution in England. And the royal couple, like their people, were unabashedly sentimental, especially during the holidays. On one occasion, they were transfixed by a flourish of midnight trumpets announcing the start of the New Year. That music, Victoria wrote in her journal, "quite affected dear Albert, who turned pale and had tears in his eyes and pressed my hand very warmly. It touched me, for I felt he must be thinking of his dear native country which he left for me."

To a woman of such feeling, charity was second nature. As one Victorian noted, "Her Majesty's Royal bounties to the poor . . . are well known, the ancient Christmas and New Year's gifts being dispensed with great generosity. . . . Then there is the distribution of the beef, a most interesting feature of the Royal Bounty."

The widespread need for alms was but one sign that the new industrial prosperity had not reached large segments of society. Even on Christmas, countless poor wretches, including children, worked long hours in the mines and factories. Never did their slum homes seem grimmer to them than on Christmas Day. And never were protests in their behalf more vociferous than at Christmas. One of the most eloquent spokesmen for humanitarian reform was the novelist Charles Dickens. His story, "A Christmas Carol," wrung honest tears from worldly intellectuals as well as greengrocers' wives. Slowly, reforms were adopted. One of these, incorporated in the Bank Holiday Act of 1871, made Christmas an official day of rest in England, and 19 years later America's last laggard, the territory of Oklahoma, followed suit.

By then, Victoria's long reign was drawing to its end. The middle-class home Christmas that emerged in her age has changed little since, except to grow even more inclusive. Yet the increased pace of life in the 20th Century fills many moderns with nostalgia for that earlier age—that warm, safe, contented time when there was leisure enough to enjoy Christmas to the full. For them, the thought of Christmas still conjures up a host of images that are distinctly Victorian: of huge family gatherings in thatch-roofed country cottages; of trim coaches and horse-drawn sleighs; of men in stovepipe hats, prim women whose skirts brush the snows, children in long, bright mufflers. These quaint scenes still adorn modern Christmas cards. And so do sentimental pictures of the "waits," those Victorian carolers who wandered the streets in small groups, ready to sing for a few pennies. In London many of them were young Cockneys, and when they burst into song their accents rang out clear:

'Ark, the 'erald h'angels sing,
Glory to the newborn King.

PLUMP MOLLY DUMPLING, *the epitome of the Victorian cook, plunges her Christmas pudding into water. After cooking, this delectable fruity mass was doused with brandy and served aflame.*

THE FINAL HALF-HOUR *before Christmas dinner is gently satirized in this Victorian print. Though grandpa snoozes, the atmosphere is tense. The children*

BRAVE FAMILIES AT THEIR FEASTING

English Victorians, looking back on Christmas banquets of the past, considered their holiday dinner quite restrained. But in setting a table to match their rising standard of living, they consumed enough to make their descendants blanch. The serious eating on Christmas Day began about 1 p.m. The typical lunch included soup, stuffed turkey, plum pudding and mince pie. Then came an elaborate tea at 5 o'clock.

The principal meal of the day—it is drolly depicted in the Victorian prints on these pages—began around 9. There was trout, a suckling pig roasted whole on the spit, candy and cake, and several kinds of wine. It

IN A FLURRY OF TOASTS, *the Christmas dinner draws to a close with mince pies and plum pudding on the table. Even baby has been brought down to share the excitement.*

tless, and relations with the help are probably strained.

took courage to face up to such a feast, and satirists like William Makepeace Thackeray chortled with glee over the disappointing dishes and the big food bills that inevitably ensued. But most Victorians enjoyed every minute and every morsel of it, and they worked off their postprandial lethargy in gay romps and games.

AFTER THE DINNER, *the young people whirl to music by their elders, while the children valiantly continue to gorge themselves and stuff their dog with the last of the goodies.*

LIGHTS
FOR EUROPE'S
MYRIAD
CELEBRATIONS

IGNITING THE YULE LOG *in a kitchen oven, the patriarch of a French family chants, "May our Lord fill us with happiness. And if next year we have not more, O God, let us not have less."*

In Western Europe in the 19th Century, the Christmas season glowed with light in celebrations that were much the same as they are today. In Spain, children carrying lamps on poles scattered through city streets to light the way for the Three Kings bearing gifts. In Italy, candles were lit at ornate crèches in churches, town squares and in fine homes draped with lemon blossoms and periwinkles. In German homes, the halls were purposefully kept dark so that the children would be dazzled as they burst into brilliantly lit rooms where candles burned on the Christmas trees *(opposite)* and presents awaited. In Sweden, lovely young girls risked singeing their hair to honor their parents *(below)*. In France, where the *bûche de Noël* (yule log) was ceremoniously ignited *(above)*, every window on Paris' great boulevards blazed with light on Christmas night and, one English visitor noted, "even the table of the poor chestnut vendor has an additional lamp." Similar customs, as well as many unique ones, had also reached their present form in Eastern Europe *(next pages)*.

A GERMAN CHRISTMAS ROOM *is a candlelit paradise. Besides toys each child received a "Bunte Teller," or plate of sweets.*

LIGHTING THE DARK, *a Swedish girl appears before her parents wearing a white dress and a bonnet of candles. She brings them music and coffee at 2 a.m. on December 13, St. Lucia's day.*

AN ARISTOCRATIC FAMILY *in 19th Century Russia examines presents around the Christmas trees. In 20th Century Russia, as in 17th Century Englan*

OLD WAYS IN EASTERN EUROPE

A pre-Christmas fast, widely and diversely observed today, had become a vital part of the holiday in Eastern Europe by the 19th Century. In Russia, no meat was served for 40 days, and on the day before Christmas, there was no food at all until the first evening star appeared. Then,

after Mass, Russians went home to feast on foods bought from peasants in open sleighs—pastrami, pigs and geese, duck and quail.

Christmas trees by the thousands went on sale in Moscow three days before the great day. Decorations for the trees and for the house were

A GOOD-LUCK CAKE *is blessed by a Serbian family, whose members cluster around it holding lighted candles. Hidden in the cake is a silver coin, said to bring good fortune to the finder.*

A BLINDFOLDED GOOSE, *turned loose at a German Christmas party, is urged on toward the oldest unmarried girl. According to legend, the girl whom the bird touches first will wed first.*

Christmas was banned for a time and then restored.

so expensive that most were home-made. Apples and tangerines were strung up, and dolls were made of dried fruit and candy. Walnuts were dipped in egg white, rolled in sheets of gold foil and hung by threads.

Old social customs and folk superstitions added charm to the festivities. On the third or fourth day of Christmas, Russian servants in aristocratic homes renewed their annual contracts with their employers or looked for new positions. In either case, the negotiations called for several drinks. Meanwhile, little work was done for reasons explained by many old sayings. It was also the season for fortunetelling, for seeing auguries of the future everywhere. To many Russians, a frosty Christmas meant a rich grain harvest next year. Starry skies promised a good crop of peas, but if the skies stayed dark, the cows would be productive.

HAPPY TRAPPERS *for the Hudson's Bay Company greet Christmas beside a roaring fire. As the others sing, one woodsman proposes a toast from his dog sled.*

NOSTALGIC COWBOYS *are shown at their revels in the 1891 Christmas issue of "Frank Leslie's" magazine. "Leslie's" entitled the picture, "Sweet, Sweet Home."*

THE HOLIDAY OUT WEST

Christmas in the American West inspired many fanciful pictures by popular artists in their city studios. But if frontier celebrations seldom included a pudding *(above),* they were often as sentimental as the artists' versions of them. Christmas sharp-

WELL-EQUIPPED HUNTERS *prepare a Christmas pudding in their wilderness camp. The deer hanging in the background probably provided suet, the main ingredient in the dessert. But few frontier hunters took to the woods with the rich fruits and spices required for a proper pudding.*

ened the yearning of pioneer families separated from old friends. In gold camps and cow towns, lonely men banged tin pans, fired their pistols, sang noisily and held all-male dances. One of three miners who spent a Christmas in camp recalled,

"I took out of my belt two heavy nuggets . . . and gave one to each of them. It was a poor enough gift. Gold was a common commodity with us. They'd have appreciated a hot biscuit a lot more."

But the West had its traditional

Christmases long before the country was fully settled. One German visitor to Texas in 1846 reported seeing "a richly decorated and illuminated Christmas tree . . . where . . . scarcely two years ago the camp fires of the wild Comanches were burning."

A LONG WINTER'S NAP

ON, DONDER AND BLITZEN

DOWN THE CHIMNEY

STRAIGHT TO HIS WORK

AN EARLY SANTA CLAUS, *seen in 1849 sketches for Moore's "A Visit from St. Nicholas," shows less bulk and cheer than the elf in the poem.*

A NEW LOOK FOR SANTA CLAUS

At the start of the 19th Century, the traditional Christmastime gift-giver was St. Nicholas, a tall, stern patriarch in bishop's robes. By the end of the century he was Santa Claus, a tubby, jovial figure in a red suit. This remarkable transformation was helped along by several writers: they gave St. Nicholas a pipe, a prosperous air, a single reindeer. But the biggest contributions were made by two of the unlikeliest men—a serious classical scholar and a famous political cartoonist.

Clement C. Moore was a professor at an Episcopal seminary in New York. He was opposed to "frivolous amusements," yet to please his children he devoted a few hours to frivolous versifying in 1822. The result was "A Visit from St. Nicholas." The poem began, "'Twas the night be-fore Christmas," and it presented as St. Nicholas a jolly, globular, sky-riding elf. Moore's St. Nicholas gradually won popularity. Then in 1862, the figure was adopted by Thomas Nast, whose vitriolic pen was the fear of many a candidate for public office. It was Nast who gave Santa his fur-trimmed outfit and who put the finishing touches on the merry old soul we know today (*opposite*).

THOMAS NAST'S SANTA CLAUS *shakes with mirth in a sketch from "Har-*
per's Weekly." This Santa was developed by 1886 and has changed little since.   189

CHRISTMAS AT HOME ON THE FARM

The gay family scene at the right is entitled *Christmas at Home.* It came from the brush of a cheerful old lady who began painting when she was 76, and who kept it up, making "a batch" of three or four pictures each week, until she was more than 100 years old. She was Anna Mary Robertson Moses, familiarly known as Grandma Moses, and her bright nostalgic scenes have made her one of the champion Christmas card artists of all time. Nearly 50 million people have received holiday wishes on the back of Grandma's prints.

The secret of her success, Grandma Moses once explained, was that "I like to paint oldtimy things—something real pretty. Most of them are daydreams, as it were." Into *Christmas at Home* she daydreamed a farmhouse parlor much like those in upper New York State and Virginia's Shenandoah Valley, where she spent most of her life. Christmas presents are still being opened and Christmas dinner is being set out on separate tables for the grownups and the children. Almost every detail of the typical farm Christmas is present in the picture—except the two things most closely associated with Christmas in Grandma's mind. One was the scent of hemlock around the Christmas tree, and the other was the smell of varnish on old toys thriftily repainted for a new Christmas.

RECITING "A CHRISTMAS CAROL," *author Dickens (above) stirs an audience to tears.*

DICKENS' CHERISHED CLASSIC

To Charles Dickens, the most popular of Victorian novelists, Christmas was "the only time I know of, in the long calendar of the year when men and women seem by one consent to open their shut-up hearts freely." It was in this spirit that Dickens, in the late fall of 1843, started writing "A Christmas Carol." He finished it in a frenzy, laughing and weeping at his desk. The story of miserly old Scrooge and Tiny Tim and all the others did not catch on immediately. But Dickens popularized it in readings (above) before audiences in England and America. The story, part of which appears on pages 196-197, became a 20th Century Christmas classic on film and radio. Some of its characters are illustrated at right and on the next pages by the celebrated English caricaturist Ronald Searle.

CHARACTERS IN THE "CAROL" *include old Scrooge (opposite page), whose chilly meanness "nipped his pointed nose"; a Christmas phantom in black (right, top); and Marley's Ghost (right, bottom), who wore "ghostly spectacles turned up on his ghostly forehead."*

THE GHOST OF CHRISTMAS YET TO COME

THE GHOST OF THE MISERABLE MARLEY

SCROOGE: "A SQUEEZING, WRENCHING, GRASPING, SCRAPING, CLUTCHING, COVETOUS OLD SINNER"

PURSUING A PRETTY LADY, *Scrooge joyfully plays blindman's buff at his nephew's Christmas party. This scene is one of the many visions that*

were shown to the old miser by the Christmas ghosts. Filled with remorse by what he has seen, Scrooge resolves to keep Christmas all year round.

THE CRATCHITS
AT
DINNER

"A Christmas Carol" by Charles Dickens (1812-1870) radiates the mood of benevolence—and sentimentality—that pervaded the Victorian Christmas. This story did as much as any single work to preserve that Victorian mood as a part of today's family Christmas. The happy scene that appears below is taken from a special version prepared by Dickens himself for public readings on his tours of England and America.

Scrooge and the Ghost passed on, invisible, straight to Scrooge's clerk's; and on the threshold of the door the Spirit smiled, and stopped to bless Bob Cratchit's dwelling with the sprinklings of his torch. Think of that! Bob had but fifteen "Bob" a week himself; he pocketed on Saturdays but fifteen copies of his Christian name; and yet the Ghost of Christmas Present blessed his four-roomed house!

Then up rose Mrs. Cratchit, Cratchit's wife, dressed out but poorly in a twice-turned gown, but brave in ribbons, which are cheap and make a goodly show for sixpence; and she laid the cloth, assisted by Belinda Cratchit, second of her daughters, also brave in ribbons; while Master Peter Cratchit plunged a fork into the saucepan of potatoes, and, getting the corners of his monstrous shirt-collar (Bob's private property, conferred upon his son and heir in honor of the day) into his mouth, rejoiced to find himself so gallantly attired, and yearned to show his linen in the fashionable Parks. And now two smaller Cratchits, boy and girl came tearing in, screaming that outside the baker's they had smelt the goose, and known it for their own; and, basking in luxurious thoughts of sage and onion, these young Cratchits danced about the table, and exalted Master Peter Cratchit to the skies, while he (not proud, although his collars nearly choked him) blew the fire, until the slow potatoes, bubbling up, knocked loudly at the saucepan-lid to be let out and peeled.

"What has ever got your precious father then?" said Mrs. Cratchit. "And your brother Tiny Tim! And Martha warn't as late last Christmas day by half an hour!"

"Here's Martha, mother!" said a girl, appearing as she spoke.

"Here's Martha, mother!" cried the two young Cratchits. "Hurrah! There's *such* a goose, Martha!"

"Why, bless your heart alive, my dear, how late you are!" said Mrs. Cratchit, kissing her a dozen times, and taking off her shawl and bonnet for her.

"We'd a deal of work to finish up last night," replied the girl, "and had to clear away this morning, mother!"

"Well! Never mind so long as you are come," said Mrs. Cratchit. "Sit ye down before the fire, my dear, and have a warm, Lord bless ye!"

"No, no! There's father coming," cried the two young Cratchits, who were everywhere at once. "Hide, Martha, hide!"

So Martha hid herself, and in came little Bob, the father, with at least three feet of comforter, exclusive of the fringe, hanging down before him; and his threadbare clothes darned up and brushed, to look seasonable; and Tiny Tim upon his shoulder. Alas for Tiny Tim, he bore a little crutch, and had his limbs supported by an iron frame!

"Why, where's our Martha?" cried Bob Cratchit, looking round.

"Not coming," said Mrs. Cratchit.

"Not coming!" said Bob, with a sudden declension in his high spirits; for he had been Tim's blood-horse all the way from church, and had come home rampant,—"not coming on Christmas day!"

Martha didn't like to see him disappointed, if it were only in joke; so she came out prematurely from behind the closet door, and ran into his arms, while the two young Cratchits hustled Tiny Tim, and bore him off into the wash-house, that he might hear the pudding singing in the copper.

"And how did little Tim behave?" asked Mrs. Cratchit, when she had rallied Bob on his credulity, and Bob had hugged his daughter to his heart's content.

"As good as gold," said Bob, "and better. Somehow he gets thoughtful, sitting by himself so much, and thinks the strangest things you ever heard. He told me, coming home, that he hoped the people saw him in the church, because he was a cripple, and it might be pleasant to them to remember, upon Christmas day, who made lame beggars walk and blind men see."

Bob's voice was tremulous when he told them this, and trembled more when he said that Tiny Tim was growing strong and hearty.

His active little crutch was heard upon the floor, and back came Tiny Tim before another word was spoken, escorted by his brother and sister to his stool beside the fire; and while Bob, turning up his cuffs,—as if, poor fellow, they were capable of being made more shabby,—compounded some hot mixture in a jug with gin and lemons, and stirred it round and round and put it on the hob to simmer, Master Peter and the two ubiquitous young Cratchits went to fetch the goose, with which they soon returned in high procession.

Mrs. Cratchit made the gravy (ready beforehand in a little saucepan) hissing hot; Master Peter mashed the potatoes with incredible vigor; Miss Belinda sweetened up the apple-sauce; Martha dusted the hot plates; Bob took Tiny Tim beside him in a tiny corner at the table; the two young Cratchits set chairs for everybody, not forgetting themselves, and mounting guard upon their posts, crammed spoons into their mouths, lest they should shriek for goose before their turn came to be helped. At last the dishes were set on, and grace was said. It was succeeded by a breathless pause, as Mrs. Cratchit, looking slowly all along the carving-knife, prepared to plunge it in the breast; but when she did, and when the long-expected gush of stuffing issued forth, one murmur of delight arose all round the board, and even Tiny Tim, excited by the two young Cratchits, beat on the table with the handle of his knife, and feebly cried, Hurrah!

There never was such a goose. Bob said he didn't believe there ever was such a goose cooked. Its tenderness and flavor, size and cheapness, were the themes of universal admiration. Eked out by apple-sauce and mashed potatoes, it was a sufficient dinner for the whole family; indeed, as Mrs. Cratchit said with great delight (surveying one small atom of a bone upon the dish), they hadn't ate it all at last! Yet every one had had enough, and the youngest Cratchits in particular were steeped in sage and onion to the eyebrows! But now, the plates being changed by Miss Belinda, Mrs. Cratchit left the room alone,—too nervous to bear witnesses,—to take the pudding up, and bring it in.

Suppose it should not be done enough! Suppose it should break in turning out! Suppose somebody should have got over the wall of the back yard, and stolen it, while they were merry with the goose,—a supposition at which the two young Cratchits became livid! All sorts of horrors were supposed.

Hallo! A great deal of steam! The pudding was out of the copper. A smell like a washing-day! That was the cloth. A smell like an eating-house and a pastry-cook's next door to each other, with a laundress's next door to that! That was the pudding! In half a minute Mrs. Cratchit entered,—flushed but smiling proudly,—with the pudding, like a speckled cannon-ball, so hard and firm, blazing in half of half a quartern of ignited brandy, and bedight with Christmas holly stuck into the top.

O, a wonderful pudding! Bob Cratchit said, and calmly too, that he regarded it as the greatest success achieved by Mrs. Cratchit since their marriage. Mrs. Cratchit said that now the weight was off her mind she would confess she had had her doubts about the quantity of flour. Everybody had something to say about it, but nobody said or thought it was at all a small pudding for a large family. Any Cratchit would have blushed to hint at such a thing. . . .

There was nothing of high mark in this. They were not a handsome family; they were not well dressed; their shoes were far from being waterproof; their clothes were scanty; and Peter might have known, and very likely did, the inside of a pawnbroker's. But they were happy, grateful, pleased with one another, and contented with the time. . . .

Christmas Eve in the Tyrol

Austrian-born Ludwig Bemelmans (1898-1962) describes the European custom of star-singing in this excerpt from his book "Hansi."

"Christmas Eve," thought Hansi, "should start with the evening. There should be no day on that day at all." Certainly it was the biggest day in the year and the longest to wait around in.

He was sent from the house on errands as soon as he came in. Packages wandered around. One room was locked and even the keyhole stuffed so one could see nothing.

The children weren't hungry though there were the most wonderful things on the table.

"Hansi, nothing is going to happen until this plate is empty. Lieserl, stop wiggling on that chair." Uncle Herman finally looked at his watch and got up. Soon a little silver bell rang, and sparkling across the hall stood the Christmas tree. It turned slowly to music, as glass angels, cookies and burning candles rode around.

The best skis in the whole world are made of Norwegian spruce with long tapered ends. Such a pair stood beside the tree—new and with a binding like that the champion jumpers use. Next to them a skiing cap with a long tassel. Aunt Amalie had knitted it for Hansi. The skis, of course, were from his mother. Uncle Herman had given Hansi a skiing jacket, bright red and warm so that one could get lost and yet stay warm and easily be found in the white snow.

Lieserl had a doll carriage with a big doll dressed like a peasant girl on Sunday. This doll could go to sleep and even said "Mamma," when she was pinched.

"Yes, Lieserl, I see," said Hansi, and looked at his skis again.

Hansi had barely slipped into the skis to try them on and put the stocking cap on his head, when singing was heard outside the house.

"Here they are," said Uncle Herman. Everybody tiptoed to the door, and quietly it swung open.

Three Kings stood majestically in the starry night and sang in verses. They told how they had come from the sands of the desert and were passing this house on the way to visit the Christ Kinderl, to offer Him their precious gifts. Long heavy robes of scarlet flowed off them into the snow. Over their serious devout faces shone tall crowns of pure gold. Their hands were hidden in the deep folds of scarlet sleeves and one of them held a silver lance on which shone the star that had guided the Kings from the East past this house.

After they had finished their song, Uncle Herman invited them to enter his home. He did so singing a verse to which they answered with singing and came in.

Aunt Amalie had brought three cups of hot chocolate and a big plate of Lebkuchen. The Kings seemed to be very hungry indeed after the hard trip from the hot desert and over the cold mountains. Each took three Lebkuchen as they sat down, falling over the plate in their hurry to reach it. One Lebkuchen was left and, as one of the Kings tried to reach for it, the biggest one hit him on the fingers with the silver lance to which was attached the morning star, which broke off and fell into the chocolate. Uncle Herman seemed to know these Kings very well. He took the lances away from them so they would not hurt each other any more.

Lieserl sat down next to the smallest King, who was black, and looked at him very closely. Then she wet her finger and rubbed his nose. The King started to cry and his nose turned white.

"I knew it all the time," said Lieserl. "It's Frau Kofler's little boy Peterl."

Now Hansi came to the table, and he could see that the King, outside of a black face, had only black fingernails. His hands were white—almost white. They were boys from the village. The beautiful stars and crowns were made of cardboard with gold and silver paper pasted over it and the little King was blackened with burnt cork.

They had to sing at three more houses, they said. Aunt Amalie brought two more Lebkuchen, so each could eat another, and Uncle Herman repaired the little King's pale nose with stove blacking. They gave thanks with a little verse for the shelter and food and bowed and walked back into the night. The cold light of the moon gave them back their lost majesty. As they left everyone was serious and quiet. Their stars and crowns had turned again to purest beaten gold.

The evening passed as quickly as the day had been slow in going. Soon it was time to go to midnight services.

This was one of three days in the year when Uncle Herman stood in front of a mirror. He buttoned his tunic and pinned his medals on according to regulation, "six fingers down from the seam of the collar, three fingers over from the second button—right over the heart." Belt and saber were adjusted carefully. Uncle Herman breathed on the buckle and polished it with his sleeve.

Aunt Amalie said, "Why don't you ask for a piece of cloth? It's a shame—the nice new uniform."

The feathers on the green huntsman's hat were straightened out, the white gloves put on.

The children looked up in awe at their new uncle who looked like a picture of his old emperor.

Aunt Amalie had her best dress on with a wide silk shawl around her shoulders and silver lacing from which jingled heavy thalers as she walked. . .

Aunt Amalie put some things on the table for a small supper when they came back.

The night helped to make Christmas. All the stars were out. The windows of the mountain church shone out into the blue night from the valley and from high up little rows of lights came towards the church. People carried them. They shone up into happy, quiet faces. Silent, holy night—only the bells of the churches rang from near and from the far white fields.

Parisian
Holiday

Paris had a brilliant Christmas in 1876 despite France's recent defeat in the Franco-Prussian War. The holiday is described below in an informal report by Henry James (1843-1916), then New York "Tribune" correspondent in Paris.

. . . But why should I talk of pictures when Paris itself, for the last few days, has formed an immense and brilliant picture. French babies, I believe, hang up their stocking—or put a shoe into the stove—on New Year's Eve; but Christmas, nevertheless, has been very good-humoredly kept. I have never seen Paris so charming as on this last Christmas Day. The weather put in a claim to a share in the fun, the sky was radiant and the air as soft and pure as a southern spring. It was a day to spend in the streets and all the world did so. I passed it strolling half over the city and wherever I turned I found the entertainment that a pedestrian relishes. What people love Paris for became almost absurdly obvious: charm, beguilement, diversion were stamped upon everything. I confess that, privately, I kept thinking of Prince Bismarck and wishing he might take a turn upon the boulevards. Not that they would have flustered him much, I suppose, for, after all, the boulevards are not human; but the whole spectacle seemed a supreme reminder of the fact so constantly present at this time to the reflective mind —the amazing elasticity of France. Beaten and humiliated on a scale without precedent, despoiled, dishonored, bled to death financially—all this but yesterday—Paris is today in outward aspect as radiant, as prosperous, as instinct with her own peculiar genius as if her sky had never known a cloud. The friendly stranger cannot refuse an admiring glance to this mystery of wealth and thrift and energy and good spirits. I don't know how Berlin looked on Christmas Day, though Christmas-keeping is a German specialty, but I greatly doubt whether its aspect would have appealed so irresistibly to the sympathies of the impartial observer. With the approach of Christmas here the whole line of the boulevards is bordered on each side with a row of little booths for the sale—for the sale of everything conceivable. The width of the classic asphalt is so ample that they form no serious obstruction, and the scene, in the evening especially, presents a picturesque combination of the rustic fair and the highest Parisian civilization. You may buy anything in the line of trifles in the world, from a cotton nightcap to an orange neatly pricked in blue letters with the name of the young lady—Adèle or Ernestine—to whom you may gallantly desire to present it. On the other side of the crowded channel the regular shops present their glittering portals, decorated for the occasion with the latest refinements of the trade. The confectioners in particular are amazing; the rows of marvelous *bonbonnières* look like precious sixteenth-century caskets and reliquaries, chiseled by Florentine artists, in the glass cases of great museums. The *bonbonnière,* in its elaborate and impertinent uselessness, is certainly the consummate flower of material luxury; it seems to bloom, with its petals of satin and its pistils of gold, upon the very apex of the tree of civilization.

A Happy Christmas to You!

OLD-FASHIONED CARDS

Modern Christmas card designs often wander far from traditional themes. In this verse from a poem entitled "Epstein, Spare that Yule Log!" American satirist Ogden Nash rushes to the defense of the time-honored holly and mistletoe.

Oh, give me an old-fashioned Christmas card,
With hostlers hostling in an old inn yard,
With church bells chiming their silver notes,
And jolly red squires in their jolly red coats,
And a good fat goose by the fire that dangles,
And a few more angels and a few less angles.
Turn backward, Time, to please this bard,
And give me an old-fashioned Christmas card.

Sounds of Singing

Bittersweet memories of childhood Christmases in an English country town are evoked here in a stream-of-consciousness poem. Its author is the contemporary English writer Leonard Clark.

I had almost forgotten the singing in the streets,
Snow piled up by the houses, drifting
Underneath the door into the warm room,
Firelight, lamplight, the little lame cat
Dreaming in soft sleep on the hearth, mother dozing,
Waiting for Christmas to come, the boys and me
Trudging over blanket fields waving lanterns to the sky.
I had almost forgotten the smell, the feel of it all,
The coming back home, with girls laughing like stars.
Their cheeks, holly berries, me kissing one,
Silent-tongued, soberly, by the long church wall;
Then back to the kitchen table, supper on the white
    cloth,
Cheese, bread, the home-made wine;
Symbols of the night's joy, a holy feast.
And I wonder now, years gone, mother gone,
The boys and girls scattered, drifted away with the
    snowflakes,
Lamplight done, firelight over,
If the sounds of our singing in the streets are still there,
Those old tunes, still praising;
And now, a life-time of Decembers away from it all,
A branch of remembering holly spears my cheeks,
And I think it may be so;
Yes, I believe it may be so.

CHURCHILL'S CHRISTMAS IN THE WHITE HOUSE

Thoughts of children at Christmas inspired the speech which Winston Churchill made to the American people during a wartime visit in 1941.

I spend this anniversary and festival far from my country, far from my family, and yet I cannot truthfully say that I feel far from home. Whether it be the ties of blood on my mother's side, or the friendships I have developed here over many years of active life, or the commanding sentiment of comradeship in the common cause of great peoples who speak the same language, who kneel at the same altars and, to a very large extent, pursue the same ideals; I cannot feel myself a stranger here in the centre and at the summit of the United States. I feel a sense of unity and fraternal association which, added to the kindliness of your welcome, convinces me that I have a right to sit at your fireside and share your Christmas joys.

Fellow workers, fellow soldiers in the cause, this

is a strange Christmas Eve. Almost the whole world is locked in deadly struggle. Armed with the most terrible weapons which science can devise, the nations advance upon each other. Ill would it be for us this Christmastide if we were not sure that no greed for the lands or wealth of any other people, no vulgar ambitions, no morbid lust for material gain at the expense of others, had led us to the field. Ill would it be for us if that were so. Here, in the midst of war, raging and roaring over all the lands and seas, sweeping nearer to our hearths and homes; here, amid all these tumults, we have tonight the peace of the spirit in each cottage home and in every generous heart. Therefore we may cast aside, for this night at least, the cares and dangers which beset us and make for the children an evening of happiness in a world of storm. Here then, for one night only, each home throughout the English-speaking world should be a brightly-lighted island of happiness and peace.

Let the children have their night of fun and laughter, let the gifts of Father Christmas delight their play. Let us grown-ups share to the full in their unstinted pleasures before we turn again to the stern tasks and the formidable years that lie before us, resolved that by our sacrifice and daring these same children shall not be robbed of their inheritance or denied their right to live in a free and decent world.

And so, in God's mercy, a happy Christmas to you all.

God Rest You Merry

One of the most popular of Christmas carols, especially in England, is reproduced below. Over the years it has been sung to at least two tunes. This familiar melody was printed and offered for sale in London as early as the 1790s.

God rest you mer-ry gen - tle men, Let no-thing you dis - may, To save us all from
Re - member Christ our Sa - vior Was born on Christmas Day,

Sa - tan's power when we were gone a - stray; O_____ ti - dings of com - fort and

joy, com-fort and joy, O_____ -ti - dings of com - fort and joy.

XV

A LIVING TRADITION

THE NATURAL TENDENCY OF time to obliterate ancient customs, and silence ancient sports, is too much promoted by the utilitarian spirit of the day; and they who would have no man enjoy, without being able to give a reason for the enjoyment which is in him, are robbing life of half its beauty, and some of its virtues. If the old festivals and hearty commemorations....had no other recommendations than their *convivial* character —the community of enjoyment which they imply—they would, on that account alone, be worthy of all promotion....We love all which tends to call man from the solitary and chilling pursuit of his own separate and selfish views, into the warmth of common sympathy, and within the bands of a common brotherhood.

"THE BOOK OF CHRISTMAS," THOMAS K. HERVEY

THE MUMMERS PARADE *in Philadelphia features elaborate costumes, as did medieval celebrations during the Christmas season.*

A PROFUSION
OF FEASTS
AND CUSTOMS

GLOWING CANDLES *illuminate the interior of Old Swede's Church, Philadelphia, during the celebration of the Lucia light festival.*

CHRISTMAS TODAY in the United States is celebrated with a multitude of traditions—some ancient, some comparatively recent; some devout, some secular; some transplanted from European homelands; a few— among Indians and Eskimos—partly indigenous.

A public observance for all the nation is the lighting of the tree on the White House lawn by the President—a custom originated by Warren G. Harding. But there is hardly an American town that does not have some Christmas observance of its own in which local citizens may actively participate. On Boston's Beacon Hill, strolling carolers converge on Louisburg Square, whose householders put candles in the windows to light the songsters' way. In Seattle, foreign communities, consulates and church groups join in presenting a festival which depicts "Christmas around the World" staged with authentic foreign costumes, music and refreshments.

"Christmas Trees around the World" is a favorite theme of similar festivals. In Dallas, for example, a

dozen trees are displayed, each one placed before a backdrop representing a custom or legend of a different country. In Atlanta the Christmas trees share a display with crèches of various nations—an Italian crèche of glass, a French Provençal crèche with carved wood figures, brilliantly decorated in paint.

Countless plays and pageants are presented. A Lutheran church in North Hollywood builds a 200-foot-long stage-set of Bethlehem; four parishioners dressed as Roman heralds on horseback announce Caesar's decree, while others in appropriate costumes play the parts of angels and shepherds. In church vestries and parish houses in every state, mothers straighten the robes of many small Wise Men, and paper-winged angels rehearse their lines.

Some events of the Christmas season have been deliberately started in emulation of old customs. Palmer Lake, Colorado, holds a Yule log hunt on the Sunday before Christmas. A four-foot log is hidden in the mountains outside town, and the finder drags it back to City Hall, where it is set afire. The Philadelphia Mummers Parade, held on New Year's Day, echoes a tradition of masked revelry that dates back to the Roman *kalends,* and that was practiced with highly elaborate costumes and wild pantomime in medieval and Renaissance festivities at Christmastime.

Many Americans still observe the customs of their ancestors from foreign lands. Polish Catholic families on Christmas Eve break and share the thin wafer called *oplatek,* a symbol of love and devotion. Moravian communities in Winston-Salem, North Carolina, and Bethlehem, Pennsylvania, continue the custom of *putz-*

ing—making tiny figures to decorate the tree—and of distributing beeswax candles at Christmas Eve services as a reminder that Christ came to be the Light of the World.

Light is the theme, too, of the Swedish Lucia Fest—the festival of St. Lucy. Eight boys carrying golden stars lead a procession into the church; then youngsters dressed as elves skip down the aisle to a pot of food left for them *(opposite).* They are followed by 30 girls in white, carrying candles. At the end comes a lovely girl dressed as Lucia, crowned with seven burning candles. And everyone sings old Swedish carols.

In Alaska, Eskimos celebrate Christmas with the feasts (reindeer roast and a dessert of foamy seal blubber with blueberries) and the games (weight lifting, broad jumping and the like) which their ancestors held in pre-Christian times to mark the winter solstice. In the Southwest, Indians have blended their ancient legends of the battle between good and evil with the Christmas story as it was taught them by Spanish missionaries. The drama that results is frequently danced out with steps from the Indians' rain and fertility rites.

Thus millions of Americans, each in his own way, observe Christmas with countless combinations of colorful customs and traditions. In many instances the celebrations are 20th Century echoes of rites practiced hundreds—and even thousands —of years ago; others are clearly modern inventions inserted into the complex texture of Christmas rejoicing. But for all who celebrate in whatever fashion, Christmas remains an occasion to enjoy friends and family, a day full of the love and generosity that the first Christmas of all inspired in man's heart.

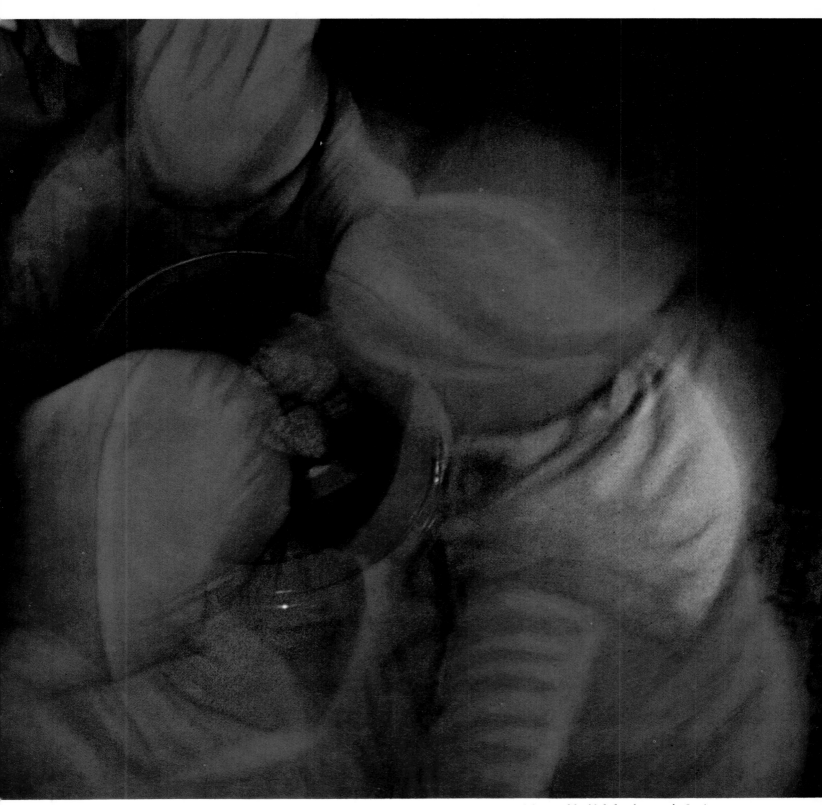

CHRISTMAS ELVES *costumed in scarlet gather around the pot of food left for them at the Lucia Fest in the Old Swede's Church in Philadelphia. The festival of St. Lucy, whose name suggests light ("lux") and whose feast day (December 13) falls close to the winter solstice when the days begin to lengthen, is a Swedish tradition widely observed in Swedish-American communities.*

ROCHESTER'S BONFIRE *lights up Twelfth Night in upstate New York. Discarded Christmas trees are piled 25 feet high and set aflame on the Lake Ontario shore. Girl Scouts sing carols and Boy Scouts throw snowballs as the holiday season ends with this gargantuan blaze.*

HOLIDAY
FIRES
AND FIREWORKS

Similarities in holiday customs often suggest connections that never existed or that have long since been lost. For example, the Chinese have for centuries celebrated their New Year with fireworks to dispel evil spirits. But in parts of the American South, where firecrackers were long used on Christmas, their only purpose was to produce a loud noise. And Williamsburg, Virginia, where Christmas is observed in the colo-

nial manner, fires its 18th Century cannon *(opposite)* simply as a parting salute to the holiday.

Similarly, many pagans of olden times and northern lands burned midwinter bonfires to speed the returning sun. Medieval Christians also burned winter bonfires, but as a practical way of disposing of holiday greenery. For the same reason —and for the fun of it, too—Christmas trees are burned today *(above)*.

WILLIAMSBURG'S GUNFIRE *marks the day after Christmas in Virginia. In the previous week, the old colonial city holds a "grand illumination," with every window candlelit.*

AT MIDNIGHT MASS *in a candlelit cave at Bethlehem, South Dakota, Catholic communicants greet the arrival of Christmas. The natural cavern, known as the Shrine of the Nativity, is reminiscent of the cave beneath the Church of the Nativity in the Holy Land's Bethlehem. The Christmas Mass is being celebrated by the prior of a Black Hills Benedictine mission on the site.*

WORSHIP,
THE HEART
OF THE HOLIDAY

In its basic character, Christmas remains deeply religious in spite of the secular festivities that have grown up around it. Christians never forget that the day commemorates the miraculous birth of a baby in whom God was incarnate. The Gospel according to St. Luke strongly suggests that Jesus was born at night. And so there arose in the Western Church, as early as 400 A.D., the custom of holding midnight Mass on Christmas Eve *(opposite)*. Earlier still, Epiphany, January 6, had been celebrated in the Eastern Orthodox Church. "Epiphany," a Greek word meaning "showing forth," refers to the three manifestations of Christ's divinity which traditionally occurred on that date: the Adoration of the Magi, His baptism by St. John, and His first miracle, the changing of water into wine at the marriage feast at Cana. To this day Epiphany remains more important to the Orthodox Churches than to others, and they celebrate it with a number of ceremonies involving water *(below)*. The third great division of Christianity, the Protestant sects, also celebrates Christ's birthday with widely divergent customs and reverent services.

IN THE LUCIA FEST, *a youthful procession in Philadelphia's Old Swede's Church is followed by a girl with a crown of candles representing Lucia (St. Lucy). This celebration of lights has been held here for 25 years.*

ON EPIPHANY, *the Greek Orthodox community of Tarpon Springs, Florida, celebrates an ancient ceremony at the water's edge. The bishop (above) blesses the waters, then throws in a cross. Young men of the congregation dive after the cross, and the one who retrieves it (right) is specially blessed.*

209

CUSTOMS ECHOING THE DISTANT PAST

YULE LOG SPRITES *bring in their contribution to the Christmas ceremony at Trinity Episcopal Cathedral, Cleveland. The practice, introduced in 1959, recalls customs established in the mists of antiquity.*

The wedding of Christian and pagan traditions at Christmas is uniquely exemplified by the Boar's Head and Yule Log ceremony of the Trinity Episcopal Cathedral in Cleveland, Ohio, pictured on these pages. The yule log tradition, believed to have come from Scandinavia, survives as proof of early Christianity's tolerance of pagan ritual. From pre-Christian times the burning of a log at the end of the year appears to have represented banishment of the old year's evil and a rekindling of the hearth fire, the center of family life. Its ashes were often scattered to bring good luck far and wide, and a part of the log was saved to light the next season's fire. The boar's head (which for the sake of convenience is sometimes represented by a suckling pig or even a pork roast) is thought by some authorities to have been eaten originally in honor of Frey, a Scandinavian deity whose symbol was the boar.

The particular ritual practiced in Cleveland has been traced back well over 100 years. It was brought to colonial America by a French Huguenot family named Bouton, who picked it up on their way through England and passed it on to a descendant. Established at the Hoosick School in Hoosick, New York, in 1888, the custom was later transplanted to Christ Church, Cincinnati, and thence to Cleveland.

The ceremony commences when a trumpeter *(opposite)* sounds three clarion calls. Costumed trenchermen carry in the boar's head on a large litter. Following them comes a group of scarlet-costumed bearers *(left)* called "sprites," who bring in the yule log. Then a soloist sings: "The boar's head in hand bear I, bedecked with bays and rosemary; and I pray you, my masters, be merry, as many as are at this feast." And the congregation responds in Latin with the following chorus: "The boar's head I bring, giving praises to God."

THE BOAR'S HEAD TRUMPETER, *standing before a stained-glass window of Cleveland's cathedral, signals the start of a Christmas procession that suggests customs of medieval England.*

INDEX

An asterisk (*) preceding a page number indicates a photograph or painting of the subject mentioned.

PART II
ANTHOLOGY SELECTIONS

CHRISTMAS MUSIC

FOR FURTHER READING

Barnett, James H., *The American Christmas.* Macmillan, 1954.

Bibles: *The New Testament Octapla,* "Eight English Versions of the New Testament in the Tyndale-King James Tradition," edited by Luther A. Weigle, Thomas Nelson and Sons, 1962; Revised Standard Version, Thomas Nelson and Sons; Douay version, Douay Bible House, 1941; The New Testament, translated by R. A. Knox, Sheed & Ward, 1954; The New Testament, edited by the Episcopal Committee of the Confraternity of Christian Doctrine, St. Anthony Guild Press, 1953.

Bornkamm, Günther, *Jesus of Nazareth.* Harper & Bros., 1961.

Burrows, Millar, *More Light on the Dead Sea Scrolls.* Viking Press, 1958.

Carpenter, Edward, *Pagan and Christian Creeds; Their Origin and Meaning.* London, George Allen & Unwin, 1921.

Chambers, E. K., *The Medieval Stage.* Oxford University Press, 1903.

Chute, Marchette, *Ben Jonson of Westminster.* E. P. Dutton & Co., 1953.

Comay, Joan, *Everyone's Guide to Israel.* Doubleday & Co., 1962.

Count, Earl W., *4,000 Years of Christmas.* Henry Schuman, 1948.

Crippen, T. C., *Christmas and Christmas Lore.* London, Blackie & Son, N. D.

Croft, Aloysius, ed., *The Mystery of Christmas.* Bruce Publishing Co., 1956.

Cullmann, Oscar, *The Early Church.* Westminster Press, 1956.

Daniel-Rops, Henri, *The Book of Mary.* Hawthorn Books, 1960.

Daniel-Rops, Henri, *Daily Life in the Time of Jesus.* Hawthorn Books, 1962.

Dawson, W. F., *Christmas: Its Origins and Associations.* London, Elliott Stock, 1902.

De Robeck, Nesta, *The Christmas Crib.* Bruce Publishing Co., 1959.

De Vaux, Roland, *Ancient Israel.* McGraw-Hill Book Co., 1961.

Evans, Joan, *Art in Mediaeval France, 987-1498.* Oxford University Press, 1948.

Ferguson, George, *Signs and Symbols in Christian Art.* Oxford University Press, 1954.

Foley, Daniel J., *Christmas in the Good Old Days.* Chilton Company, 1961.

Frazer, Sir James George, *The Golden Bough.* Macmillan, 1923.

Freeman, Margaret B., *The Story of the Three Kings* (originally written by John of Hildesheim in the 14th Century). Metropolitan Museum of Art, 1955.

Fremantle, Anne, *A Treasury of Early Christianity.* Mentor Books, 1960.

Frost, Lesley, *Come Christmas.* Coward-McCann, 1929.

Fuller, Reginald H., *The New Testament in Current Study.* Charles Scribner's Sons, 1962.

Grabar, André, and Carl Nordenfalk, *Early Medieval Painting.* Skira, 1957.

Grant, Robert M., *The Earliest Lives of Jesus.* Harper & Bros., 1961.

Greene, Richard L., *A Selection of English Carols.* Oxford University Press, 1962.

Hadfield, Miles and John, *The Twelve Days of Christmas.* Little, Brown & Co., 1962.

Harrison, Michael, *The Story of Christmas.* London, Odhams Press, N.D.

Hervey, Thomas K., *The Book of Christmas.* London, William Spooner, 1836.

Hole, Christina, *Christmas and its Customs.* M. Barrows & Co., 1958.

Hottes, Alfred Carl, *1001 Christmas Facts and Fancies.* A.T. de la Mare Company, 1954.

Huizinga, J., *The Waning of the Middle Ages.* London, Arnold, 1924.

Hutchinson, Paul, & Winfred E. Garrison, *20 Centuries of Christianity.* Harcourt, Brace and Co., 1959.

Irving, Washington, *The Sketch Book.* Dodd Mead, 1954.

Jacobus de Voragine, *The Golden Legend.* Longmans, Green & Co., 1948.

James, M. R., *The Apocryphal New Testament.* Oxford University Press, 1955.

Jobé, Joseph, *Ecce Homo.* Harper & Row, 1962.

Kane, Harnett T., *The Southern Christmas Book.* Rand McKay, 1958.

Krythe, Mamie R., *All About Christmas.* Harper & Bros., 1954.

Lewis, D. B. Wyndham, & G. C. Heseltine, *A Christmas Book, An Anthology for Moderns.* E. P. Dutton & Co., 1951.

Mâle, Emile, *Religious Art from the Twelfth to the Eighteenth Century.* Pantheon, 1949.

May, Herbert G., ed., *Oxford Bible Atlas.* Oxford University Press, 1962.

Miles, Clement A., *Christmas in Ritual and Tradition.* London, T. Fisher Unwin, 1912.

Morey, Charles Rufus, *Early Christian Art.* Princeton University Press, 1953.

Muilenberg, James, *The Way of Israel.* Harper & Row, 1961.

Puech, H. C., and other translators, *The Gospel According to Thomas.* Harper & Bros., 1959.

Rice, D. Talbot, *The Beginnings of Christian Art.* Abingdon Press, 1957.

Runciman, Steven, *A History of the Crusades.* Cambridge University Press, 1951.

Sandys, William, *Christmastide, its History, Festivities and Carols.* London, John Russell Smith, N.D.

Sechrist, Elizabeth Hough, and Janette Woolsey, *It's Time for Christmas.* Macrae Smith Company, 1959.

Sheed, F. J., ed., *The Mary Book.* Sheed & Ward, 1950.

Shoemaker, Alfred L., *Christmas in Pennsylvania.* Pennsylvania Folklife Society, 1959.

Shrady, M. L., ed., *In the Spirit of Wonder.* Pantheon Books, 1961.

Spicer, Dorothy, *Festivals of Western Europe.* H. W. Wilson Co., 1958.

Swedish Christmas. Compiled and issued by Ewert Cagner in cooperation with Goran Axel-Nilsson and Henrik Sandblad, Tre Tryckare, Gothenburg, 1955.

Tillich, Paul, *The New Being.* Charles Scribner's Sons, 1955.

Timmermans, Felix, *The Christ Child in Flanders.* Henry Regnery, 1960.

Vloberg, Maurice, *Les Noels de France.* Paris, B. Arthaud, 1953.

Weiser, Francis X., *The Christmas Book.* Harcourt Brace, 1952.

Wernecke, Herbert H., *Celebrating Christmas Around the World.* Westminster Press, 1962.

PICTURE CREDITS

Illustrations on each page are listed from left to right and from top to bottom. In the case of paintings and works of sculpture, the artist's name, if known, is given in capitals—e.g., FRA ANGELICO; the name of the photographer or the picture agency appears in parentheses—e.g., (Eric Schaal).

Page 6: The Four Evangelists, Gospel Book of Charlemagne, French, illuminated Eighth Century by GODESSALC, Rhenane School, Bibliothèque Nationale, Paris. 8—Isaiah from the high altar, 18th Century Benedictine Church at Zwiefalten, Germany (Walter Sanders). 10—Tree of Jesse, Psalter, English, 13th Century. M. 43, Pierpont Morgan Library, New York. 11—Tree of Jesse, Psalter of Ingeborg, French, 13th Century. Musée Condé, Chantilly (William J. Sumits). 12, 13—Efrem Ilani, map by Fritz Kredel. 14, 15—Manouq, David Rubinger. 16, 17—Fritz Schlesinger. 18, 19—Dmitri Kessel. 20—Drawing by Nicholas Solovioff. 21—Woodcuts by Fritz Kredel. 22—Detail, Annunciation to the Virgin, St. Columba Altarpiece, 15th Century. ROGIER VAN DER WEYDEN, Alte Pinakothek, Munich (Joachim Blauel). 24—The Annunciation, 15th Century. Veronese miniature, Budapest Museum of Fine Arts (Harry N. Abrams, Inc., New York). 25—Annunciation to the Virgin, 15th Century. FRA ANGELICO, Diocesan Museum, Cortona, Italy (Eric Schaal). 26, 27—Merode Altarpiece, 15th Century. MASTER OF FLEMALLE, Metropolitan Museum of Art, The Cloisters Collection, Purchase. 28, 29—Details from Merode Altarpiece (Dmitri Kessel). 30—Drawings by Nicholas Solovioff. 31—Woodcuts by Fritz Kredel. 32—Nativity, 13th Century. French, Chartres Cathedral, France (Dmitri Kessel). 34—Christ Child Adoration, Miniature from Book of Hours, French, 15th Century. MS. 288, Walters Art Gallery, Baltimore. 35—Adoration of the Infant, 15th Century illumination from *The Golden Legend* by Jacobus de Voragine, Bibliothèque Nationale, Paris. 36—Vierge Dorée, 13th Century. Amiens Cathedral, France (Howard Schurek). 37—Madonna and Child, Seventh Century, Church of Santa Maria Novella (Santa Francesca), Rome (James Whitmore for TIME). 38—Garden of Paradise, MASTER OF THE UPPER RHINE, early 15th Century, Städelsches Kunstinstitut, Frankfurt, Germany (Joachim Blauel). 39—Madonna Enthroned, early 15th Century. JAN VAN EYCK, Gemäldegalerie, Staatliche Kunstsammlungen, Dresden, Germany (Larry Burrows). 40—Bulto from Watrous, New Mexico, 19th Century. Taylor Museum of the Colorado Springs Fine Arts Center (L. H. Benschneider), Round woodcarving, 20th Century. DAVID CHITUKU (Society for the Propagation of the Bible, London). 41—The Nativity, JON LU HUNG HIEN, Catholic University, Peking (Dr. W. B. Pettus). 42, 43—18th Century Neapolitan Crèche (David Lees for TIME). 47—Woodcuts by Fritz Kredel. 48—Choir of Angels, late 15th Century. BENOZZO GOZZOLI, Medici-Ricardi Palace, courtesy Superintendent of Florence Art Galleries (Fernand Bourges). 50, 51—Rejoicing Angel, Marginal medallion from French Book of Hours, early 15th Century. MS. 288, Walters Art Gallery, Choir of Five Angels, Detail from the Nativity, late 15th Century. PIERO DELLA FRANCESCA, National Gallery, London (Dmitri Kessel). 52, 53—Three Angels with Instruments, Frame of center panel, Linaioli Altarpiece, early 15th Century. FRA ANGELICO, Museum of San Marco, Florence (Scala, Florence). 54, 55—Freudenaltar, late 15th Century. MASTER ARNT, Church of St. Nicholas, Calcar, Germany (Landesbildstelle, Düsseldorf). 56, 57—Drawings by Nicholas Solovioff. 59—Woodcuts by Fritz Kredel. 60—Annunciation to the Shepherds, early 15th Century. MEISTER DER GOLDENEN TAFEL, Landesmuseum, Hanover (Hans Nölter). 62—Annunciation to the Shepherds, 15th Century. Miniature from St. George's Script No. 28, Badische Landesbibliothek, Karlsruhe, Germany. 63—Annunciation to the Shepherds, 15th Century. SANO DI PIETRO, Siena Pinacoteca, Siena, Italy (Scala, Florence). 64—Kalendrier des Bergiers, Paris 15th Century. Bibliothèque Nationale, Paris (New York Public Library). 65—Annunciation to the Shepherds, Grandes Heures de la Famille de Rohan, MS. Lat. 9471, Bibliothèque Nationale, Paris. 66, 67—Adoration of the Shepherds, Dutch woodcarving, end of 15th Century. Rijksmuseum, Amsterdam (Foto-Commissie), Adoration of the Shepherds, late 15th Century. CARLO CRIVELLI, Strasbourg Museum, France (Larry Burrows for TIME). 69—Woodcuts by Fritz Kredel. 70—Procession of the Magi, late 15th Century. BENOZZO GOZ-

ZOLI, Medici-Ricardi Palace, courtesy Superintendent of Florence Art Galleries (Fernand Bourges). 72—Meeting of the Three Kings, early 15th Century. Miniature from the Très Riches Heures du Duc de Berry, Musée Condé, Chantilly (Giraudon). 73—Journey of the Three Kings, Detail of Tympanum, Southwest portal, Ulm Cathedral, Evangelisches Dekanatsamt (Dmitri Kessel). 74—Adoration of the Magi, late 13th Century. PIETRO CAVALLINI, Santa Maria in Trastevere, Rome (Scala, Florence). 75—Detail of Gifts from Adoration of the Magi, unknown painter, Dutch School, c. 1500. Kaiser Wilhelm Museum, Krefeld, Germany (Hein Engelskirchen)—drawing by Eva Cellini. 76, 77—Adoration of the Magi, late 15th Century. SANDRO BOTTICELLI, National Gallery of Art, Washington, D.C., Mellon Collection (Beck Engraving Co.). 78, 79—Sleep of the Three Kings, 12th Century. GISLEBERTUS, Cathedral of St.-Lazare, Autun, France, courtesy *Gislebertus, Sculptor of Autun*—Orion Press and *The Story of the Wise Men*—Young Scott (Franceschi Trianon Press). 80 through 84—Illustrations from "Leben der Heiligen drei Königen" in the Pierpont Morgan Library, from *The Story of the Three Kings*—*Melchior-Balthasar-Jaspar* by John of Hildesheim retold by Margaret B. Freeman. The Metropolitan Museum of Art, New York. 85—Woodcuts by Fritz Kredel. 86—Christ's Ascension, early 14th Century. GIOTTO, Arena Chapel, Padua, Italy, courtesy Superintendent of Monuments, Venice (Fernand Bourges and Robert Kafka). 88—Christ's Entry into Jerusalem, miniature from The Urbino Bible, St. Louis University. 89—Head of Christ, 1931. GEORGES ROUAULT, Cleveland Museum of Art. 90, 91—Interior Wings, Isenheim Altar, MATTHIAS GRÜNEWALD, Unterlinden Museen of Colmar, France (Eric Schaal). 92, 93—Life of Christ, COLOGNE MASTER, Staatliches Museen, Berlin-Dahlem, (Raymond and Raymond, Inc.). 94, 95—The Seven Joys of Mary, 15th Century. HANS MEMLING, Alte Pinakothek, Munich (Joachim Blauel). 96—Drawing by Nicholas Solovioff. 97—Woodcuts by Fritz Kredel. 98—Garry Winogrand. 100—Kenneth Hine. 101, 102—John De Visser. 103—Dennis Hallinan from Free Lance Photographers Guild. 104, 105—Emil Schulthess from Black Star. 106, 107—Dan Budnik from Magnum, Kosti Ruohamaa from Black Star.

Page 110—St. Nicholas, early 15th Century miniature from *The Belles Heures of Jean, Duke of Berry*. Courtesy The Metropolitan Museum of Art, The Cloisters Collection, New York, Purchase, 1954 (Robert Crandall). 112—Madonna of Mercy, Eighth Century painting, Church of Santa Maria in Trastevere, Rome (David Lees). 114—Christian symbols from carved marble slab, St. Callisto Catacombs, Rome (Pontificia Commissione di Archeologia Sacra). 115—Christ as the Sun God Helios, Early Christian mosaic from the Christian Mausoleum of the Vatican Grotto beneath St. Peter's, Rome (N. R. Farbman). 116, 117—The Four Magi, Fourth Century fresco from the Catacombs of Domitilla, Rome (Pontificia Commissione di Archeologia Sacra)—Orant, Third Century fresco from the Catacombs of Domitilla, Rome (Pontificia Commissione di Archeologia Sacra). 118, 119—Two panels from FRA ANGELICO's Altarpiece of St. Nicholas of Bari, painted in 1437 for the Cathedral of San Domenico in Perugia, Italy, now in the Pinacoteca Vaticana, Rome (Istituto d'Arti Grafiche, Bergamo)—Saint Lucy, detail from Procession of Virgin Martyrs, Sixth Century mosaic in the Basilica of Saint Apollinare Nuovo, Ravenna, Italy (Dmitri Kessel), third panel from FRA ANGELICO's Altarpiece of Saint Nicholas of Bari, now in Galleria Nazionale dell'Umbria, Perugia, Italy (Scala, Florence). 121—Woodcuts by Fritz Kredel. 122—King Edgar's Foundation Charter, title page from the 10th Century New Minster Charter, MS Cotton Vesp. A. viii, Courtesy British Museum, London. 124—King Arthur's Round Table, Winchester Castle, by permission of the Hampshire County Council (Alan Clifton). 125—King Arthur and his Knights, 14th Century miniature from *La Quête du Saint Graal et la Mort d'Arthur*, by GAUTIER MAP, Courtesy Bibliothèque Nationale, Paris (Pierre Belzeaux from Rapho Guillumette). 126—Baptism of Clovis and Coronation of Charlemagne, two 14th Century miniatures from *Les Grandes Chroniques du Saint-Denis*, Courtesy Bibliothèque Nationale, Paris (Pierre Belzeaux from Rapho Guillumette). 127—Month of December from a late-14th Century calendar, MS Rawl. D.939, Courtesy Bodleian Library, Oxford. 128, 129—Capture of Jerusalem and Crowning of King of Jerusalem, two 14th Century miniatures from *Chronique d'Outremer* by GODEFROI DE BOUILLON, MS Français 352, Courtesy Bibliothèque Nationale, Paris. 131—Woodcuts by Fritz Kredel. 132—January, 15th Century miniature from *Très Riches Heures du Duc de Berry*, Courtesy Musée Condé, Chantilly (Fernand Bourges). 134—Le Gâteau de Rois, detail of 15th Century miniature from *Heures d'Adélaïde de Savoie*, Courtesy Musée Condé, Chantilly (Photo Giraudon). 135—Boar Hunt, 15th Century French miniature, Courtesy The Wildenstein Foundation, Inc. (Frank Lerner for TIME). 136—*Le Roi Charles VII en Mage*, 15th Century miniature from *Heures d'Etienne Chevalier* by JEAN FOUQUET, MS 187, Courtesy Musée Condé, Chantilly (Photo Giraudon)—Mummers, marginal decoration from 14th Century Flemish manuscript, *Romance of Alexander the Great*, MS Bodley 264, Courtesy Bodleian Library, Oxford. 137—St. George and the Dragon, 15th Century miniature from *The Belles Heures of Jean, Duke of Berry*, Courtesy The Metropolitan Museum of Art, The Cloisters Collection, New York, Purchase, 1954 (Robert Crandall). 138, 139—Tournament, 15th Century miniature from *Chronique du Hainaut* by JACQUES DE GUISSE. Courtesy Bibliothèque Royale, Brussels (Frank Scherschel), King John, 14th Century miniature from *Chronicle of Peter Langtoft*, MS Royal 20 A II, Courtesy The British Museum, London (Larry Burrows)—Jousting, 15th Century miniature from *The Luttrel Psalter*, Courtesy The British Museum, London (Frank Scherschel). 140—St. Francis preaching to the birds, 14th Century stained glass window from Königsfelden, Switzerland, Courtesy Christophorus Verlag Herder, Freiburg/Breisgau. 141—Miracle Play, Plate 22 from Volume Nine of Josef Gregor's *Monumenta Scenica*, published in Vienna by the Management of the National Library with the support of the Society for the Publicaton of Monuments of the Theatre (Eric Schaal). 142—*Christkindwiege*, 15th Century rocking cradle from South Germany, Courtesy Bayerisches Nationalmuseum, Munich. 143—Meister Heinrich Frauenlob's Music School, 14th Century miniature from the Manessa Codex, MS 848, Courtesy Heidelberg University Library. 145—Woodcuts by Fritz Kredel. 146—German Christmas tree, 16th Century colored parchment, Courtesy Germanisches Nationalmuseum, Nuremberg. 148, 149—Henry VIII and his jester Will Somers, from a Psalter written for Henry VIII by IOHANNES MALLARD, Courtesy The British Museum, London, Queen Elizabeth and the Earl of Leicester dancing, 16th Century oil painting by an unknown artist, by kind permission of Viscount De L'Isle V.C., G.C.M.G., G.C.V.O. from his Penshurst Place Collection (Derek Bayes). 150, 151—INIGO JONES's pen and ink wash sketches for *Oberon* and colored sketch for *Hymen*, Devonshire Collection, Chatsworth. Reproduced by permission of the Trustees of the Chatsworth Settlement (Derek Bayes). 152—*Twelfth Night Feast*, 17th Century oil painting by JAN STEEN, Courtesy Museum of Fine Arts, Boston. 153—*The Feast of St. Nicholas*, 17th Century oil painting by JAN STEEN, Courtesy Rijksmuseum, Amsterdam. 154—Contemporary cast from 17th Century German cake mold, Courtesy Germanisches Nationalmuseum, Nuremberg. 155—Early 17th Century Norwegian wall hanging from Lome in the County of Christian, Courtesy Nordic Museum, Stockholm. 159—Indian, watercolor by FERDINAND BADIN, Courtesy Buffalo Historical Society, Buffalo. 161—Woodcuts by Fritz Kredel. 162—*Assembly at Wanstead House*, 18th Century oil painting, WILLIAM HOGARTH, Courtesy Philadelphia Museum of Art, Philadelphia, John Howard McFadden Collection (Fernand Bourges). 164, 165—18th Century marionettes owned by the Grimani Family at Cà Rezzonico, Venice (David Lees). 166, 167—*Knecht Ruprecht*, copper engraving by FRANZ REGIS GOZ, 1784, *Twelfth Night Waits*, 18th Century oil painting by CORNELIS TROOST, Courtesy Royal Cabinet of Paintings, The Hague. 168—18th Century Nuremberg Christmas Market, Courtesy Germanisches Nationalmuseum, Nuremberg. 169—Drawing of Moravian Love Feast Service, dated 1757, Courtesy Old Salem, Inc. 170—*High Life Below Stairs*, by ROBERT CRUIKSHANK, Courtesy The Mansell Collection. 175—Woodcuts by Fritz Kredel. 176—Victorian Christmas card, Courtesy Victoria and Albert Museum, London (Derek Bayes). 178—*The Christmas Wine*, by RALPH CALDICOTT, Courtesy The Mansell Collection, London (Derek Bayes). 179—*Christmas Plum Pudding*, by SEYMOUR, Courtesy The Mansell Collection, London (Derek Bayes). 180, 181—*The Half Hour before Dinner*, unknown artist, *The Christmas Dinner*, by SEYMOUR—*Christmas*, by GEORGE CRUIKSHANK, Courtesy The Mansell Collection, London (Derek Bayes). 182—*Weinacht ist da*, German print c. 1850 (Historia Photo). 183—*Bénédiction de la Bûche en Alsace*, Courtesy Editions B. Arthaud, Grenoble—*Lucia*, pen and ink drawing by FRITZ VAN DARDEL, Courtesy Nordic Museum, Stockholm. 184, 185—Christmas celebration in Russia c. 1860 (The Bettmann Archive), Serbian Christmas cake, 1875 (Culver Pictures)—*Christmas Oracle in Swabia*, 19th Century drawing by LOUIS BRAUN (Historisches Bildarchiv). 186, 187—Culver Pictures. 188—Illustrations from "A Visit to St. Nicholas" from *The Evergreen*, December 1849, Courtesy The New-York Historical Society, New York. 189—"Santa Claus," THOMAS NAST's drawing for *Harper's Weekly*, c. 1865, Courtesy The New-York Historical Society, New York. 190, 191—*Christmas at Home* by GRANDMA MOSES, (c) Grandma Moses Properties, Inc., Courtesy Galerie St. Etienne, New York. 192 through 196—*Charles Dickens' Last Reading* (Radio Times Hulton Picture Library), Illustrations from "A Christmas Carol" by RONALD SEARLE, Copyright (c) 1960 by Ronald Searle. By permission of the World Library. 200—Sy Seidman. 201—Woodcuts by Fritz Kredel. 202—Robert Phillips. 204—Fred Ward from Black Star. 205—Michel Lambeth. 206, 207—Michel Lambeth, Robert Phillips. 208—A. Y. Owen. 209—Fred Ward from Black Star—Flip Schulke from Black Star. 210, 211—Michel Lambeth.

ACKNOWLEDGMENTS

The editors of this volume are particularly indebted to Monsignor Myles M. Bourke, Professor of New Testament, St. Joseph's Seminary, Dunwoodie, Yonkers, New York, Professor W. D. Davies, Edward Robinson Professor of Biblical Theology, Union Theological Seminary, New York, New York, and Professor Earl W. Count, Chairman of the Department of Anthropology, Hamilton College, for their help in the preparation of the text; to Byron Dobell, who initiated the project and saw it through its earliest stages; and to Daniel Longwell, former Chairman of the Board of Editors of LIFE. In the early planning the editors were also assisted by the perceptive comments of Dr. Tom F. Driver, Union Theological Seminary, Monsignor Timothy J. Flynn, Archdiocese of New York, Professor Henri M. Peyre, Yale University, and Dr. J. Carter Swaim, Department of the English Bible, National Council of the Churches of Christ in the U.S.A. The editors are also grateful to the Reverend Lowrie John Daly, S. J., of St. Louis University, Brother William J. Kiefer, S. M., John Hadfield, J. A. R. Pimlott, Randolph E. Haugan, Margaret Reynolds and Bernice E. Leary, all of whom generously made available the results of their extensive research into the history of Christmas; to Frederick B. Adams Jr., Director, Pierpont Morgan Library; the Library of Congress Prints and Photographs Division; the New York Public Library; Bettmann Archive, Inc.; Culver Pictures, Inc.; the New-York Historical Society; the Howard University Library; the Frick Art Reference Library; the Walters Art Gallery, Baltimore; The Metropolitan Museum of Art, New York; the Victoria and Albert Museum, London; the numerous European museums, libraries and art galleries cited in the credits on pages 218, 219; and the many other individuals who contributed valuable assistance.

Grateful acknowledgment is made for permission to reprint, in whole or in part, selections from the following:

P. 20 *The Prophets*, Abraham J. Heschel. Harper & Row, Publishers, Inc., New York, 1962.

P. 30 "On the Annunciation of Fra Angelico," Manuel Machado. Translated from the Spanish by Thomas Walsh. Reprinted by permission of Mrs. Edward M. Walsh.

The Christ Child in Flanders, Felix Timmermans. Copyright 1960. The Henry Regnery Company, Chicago.

P. 31 "Annunciation to Mary," Rainer Maria Rilke. From *Translations from the Poetry of Rainer Maria Rilke*. M. D. Herter Norton. Copyright © 1938 by W. W. Norton & Company, Inc. By permission of W. W. Norton & Company, Inc., New York, and Hogarth Press, London.

English translation of lyrics for "The Angel Gabriel" from the *University Carol Book*, edited by Eric Routley, copyright 1961 by H. Freeman and Co., Brighton, England; permission granted by Mills Music Inc. for U.S.A. and Canada.

P. 44 "The Gospel of James." From *The Apocryphal Gospels*. B. Harris Cowper. Williams and Norgate, London, 1870. By permission of Ernest Benn, Ltd., London.

"A Gothic Noel," Jehan Le Povremoyne. Translated and adapted from the French by permission of the author.

P. 56 "An Iconography of Heavenly Beings," Gilbert Highet. From *Horizon* Magazine, copyright 1960 by American Heritage Publishing Company, Inc.

P. 57 "Christmas Eve," Robert Bridges. Reprinted by permission of The Clarendon Press, Oxford.

P. 58 Introduction to *The Shepherd Who Missed the Manger*, Rufus M. Jones. By permission of the Girard Trust Corn Exchange Bank, Philadelphia, Executors of the Estate of Rufus M. Jones.

Dream Days, Kenneth Grahame. By permission of the Kenneth Grahame Estate and the Bodley Head, London.

P. 68 "The Gospel of Pseudo-Matthew." From *The Apocryphal Gospels*, B. Harris Cowper. Williams and Norgate, London, 1870. By permission of Ernest Benn, Ltd., London.

"The Friendly Beasts," 12th Century English carol. Adaptation copyright, 1958, by G. Schirmer, Inc. Reprinted by permission.

"Le Grant Kalendrier des Bergiers." From *A Christmas Book: An Anthology for Moderns*, compiled by D. B. Wyndham Lewis and G. C. Heseltine. Published by E. P. Dutton & Company, Inc., New York and reprinted with their permission. Reprinted also with permission of J. M. Dent & Sons, Ltd., London.

P. 69 English translation of lyrics for "The Carol of the Bagpipers" from the *University Carol Book*, edited by Eric Routley, copyright 1961 by H. Freeman and Co., Brighton, England; permission granted by Mills Music Inc. for U.S.A. and Canada.

P. 80 *The Story of the Three Kings*, Margaret B. Freeman. Copyright 1955, The Metropolitan Museum of Art, New York.

P. 82 "Journey of the Magi," from *Collected Poems 1909-1935* by T. S. Eliot, copyright 1936, by Harcourt, Brace & World, Inc. Reprinted by permission of the publishers, and by permission of Faber and Faber, Ltd., Publishers, London.

P. 83 "Nicolas Roi Mage." From *Vent de Terre*, Roger Vercel. Translated and adapted with permission from the publisher, Editions Albin Michel, Paris.

P. 84 "Frankincense and Myrrh," copyright by Heywood Hale Broun. Reprinted by permission of Heywood Hale Broun and Constance Broun.

P. 85 "The Golden Carol" from the collection *Noels* by Marx and Anne Oberndorfer, copyright 1932, H. T. FitzSimons Company, Chicago.

P. 96 *Jerusalem and Rome: The Writings of Josephus*, selected and introduced by Nahum N. Glatzer, copyright 1960 by The World Publishing Company. By permission of Meridian Books, The World Publishing Company, Cleveland and New York.

"The Letter of Lentulus." From *The Apocryphal Gospels*, B. Harris Cowper. Williams and Norgate, London, 1870. By permission of Ernest Benn, Ltd., London.

The Dramatic History of the Christian Faith, J. J. van der Leeuw. The Theosophical Publishing House, Madras, 1927.

P. 113 From *The Ecclesiastical History of the English Nation, and Other Writings*, by The Venerable Bede. Texts by J. Stevens and John Stevenson. Everyman's Library. Reprinted by permission of E. P. Dutton & Co., Inc., New York, and J. M. Dent & Sons, Ltd., London.

P. 120 From *Times Three* by Phyllis McGinley, copyright (c) 1958 by Phyllis McGinley. Reprinted by permission of The Viking Press, Inc., New York, and Martin Secker and Warburg, Ltd., London.

Pp. 130-131 From *A Christmas Book: An Anthology for Moderns*, compiled by D. B. Wyndham Lewis and G. C. Heseltine. Published by E. P. Dutton & Co., Inc., New York, and J. M. Dent & Sons, Ltd., London, and reprinted with their permission.

P. 133 From *The Yorkist Age* by Paul Murray Kendall. Copyright (c) 1962 by Paul Murray Kendall. Reprinted by permission of W. W. Norton & Company, Inc., New York, and George Allen & Unwin, Ltd., London.

P. 144 *The Journal of Christopher Columbus*, translated by Cecil Jane. Copyright 1960 by Clarkson N. Potter, Inc., New York. Reprinted by permission of Clarkson N. Potter, Inc., and Anthony Blond, Ltd., London.

Pp. 144-145 *The Shorter Cambridge Medieval History*, by C. W. Previté-Orton Volume II. Published by the Syndics of the Cambridge University Press, New York and London, 1952.

Pp. 156-157 *Shakespeare's Christmas Gift to Queen Bess in the Year 1596*, by Anna Benneson McMahan. Published by A. C. McClurg & Co., Chicago, 1907. Reprinted with permission.

Pp. 158-159 *The Gentleman of Renaissance France*, by W. L. Wiley. Published by Harvard University Press, Cambridge, copyright 1954.

P. 161 English translation of lyrics for 'Twas in the Moon of Wintertime" (Huron Indian Carol) used by permission of the Copyright Owner, The Frederick Harris Music Co. Ltd., Oakville, Ontario.

P. 172 *Christmas with the Washingtons*, by Olive Bailey, drawings by Worth Bailey, published by The Dietz Press, Inc., Richmond, 1948. Reprinted with permission.

Pp. 198-199 From *Hansi* by Ludwig Bemelmans. Copyright (c) 1934, 1962 by Ludwig Bemelmans. Reprinted by permission of The Viking Press, Inc., New York.

P. 200 From *Verses from 1929 On* by Ogden Nash. Copyright 1933 by Ogden Nash. Reprinted by permission of Little, Brown & Company, Boston, and J. M. Dent & Sons, Ltd., London.